It's another Quality Book from CGP

This book is for anyone doing Edexcel Modular GCSE Mathematics at Higher Level.

It contains lots of tricky questions designed to make you sweat — because that's the only way you'll get any better.

It's also got some daft bits in to try and make the whole experience at least vaguely entertaining for you.

What CGP is all about

Our sole aim here at CGP is to produce the highest quality books — carefully written, immaculately presented and dangerously close to being funny.

Then we work our socks off to get them out to you — at the cheapest possible prices.

Contents

Unit Two

Probability 1
Mean, Median, Mode, Range 5
Frequency Tables 7
Grouped Frequency 9
Cumulative Frequency 10
Histograms 12
Histograms and Dispersion 13
Scatter Graphs 15
Pie Charts 16
Sampling Methods 17
Time Series 19

Unit Three

Types of Number 20
Multiples, Factors and Primes 21
Fractions and Decimals 23
Sequences 24
Calculator Buttons 26
Conversion Factors and Metric & Imperial Units 27
Rounding Off & Estimating 29
Speed 30
Density 31
Powers and Roots 32
Standard Index Form 34
Basic Algebra 35
Algebraic Fractions & D.O.T.S. 36
Algebraic Fractions 37
Perimeters and Areas 38
Volumes 39
Solids and Nets 40
Geometry 41
2D and 3D Coordinates 43
Straight Line Graphs 44

Unit Four

Surds Mostly 46
Ratios 47
Calculations — Upper Bounds and Powers 48
Fractions 49
Percentages 50
D/T Graphs and V/T Graphs 52
Regular Polygons 53
Circle Geometry 55
Surface Area and Volume 58
Loci and Constructions 60
Congruence, Similarity and Enlargement 62
Symmetry 63
The Four Transformations 65
Pythagoras and Bearings 67
Pythagoras and Coordinates 68
Trigonometry 69
The Sine and Cosine Rules 71
3D Pythagoras and Trigonometry 73
Vectors 74
Real-Life Vectors 75
$y = mx + c$ 76
Graphs to Recognise 78
Solving Equations Using Graphs 80
Simultaneous Equations and Graphs 81
The Graphs of Sin, Cos and Tan 82
Graphs: Shifts and Stretches 84
Solving Equations 86
Rearranging Formulas 88
Inequalities 90
Factorising Quadratics 92
The Quadratic Formula 93
Completing the Square 94
Trial and Improvement 95
Simultaneous Equations 96
Compound Growth and Decay 97
Direct and Inverse Proportion 99

Throughout the book, the more challenging questions are marked like this: **Q1** .

Published by Coordination Group Publications Ltd.
Illustrated by Lex Ward and Ashley Tyson

Contributors:
Gill Allen
JE Dodds
Mark Haslam
C McLoughlin
John Waller
Dave Williams

Updated by:
Simon Little, Ali Palin and Ed Robinson

With thanks to Dominic Hall *and* Vicky Daniel *for the proofreading.*

ISBN: 978 1 84146 560 9

Groovy website: www.cgpbooks.co.uk

Printed by Elanders Hindson Ltd, Newcastle upon Tyne.
Clipart sources: CorelDRAW® and VECTOR.

Text, design, layout and original illustrations © Richard Parsons 2006
All rights reserved.

UNIT TWO

Probability

Probability can be a bit of a struggle — here's a quick reminder of the basics...

PROBABILITIES are always between 0 and 1

1) You should express probabilities as a <u>fraction</u> or a <u>decimal</u>.
2) A probability of <u>ZERO</u> means that it will <u>definitely not</u> happen.
3) A probability of <u>ONE</u> means it will <u>definitely</u> happen.

Q1 The number line opposite is a <u>probability scale</u>. Place the letters where you think the following statements lie, in terms of the <u>chance</u> of the event happening.

a) The probability of getting a <u>head</u> on a toss of a 10p piece.
b) The probability of <u>choosing a red ball</u> from a bag containing 2 red balls and 1 green ball.
c) The probability of shaking a <u>five</u> on an ordinary dice.
d) The probability of choosing a <u>Guatemalan stamp</u> from a bag containing 60 British stamps and 40 French stamps.

Q2 In a game of Bingo what are the chances of pulling out the <u>15</u> ball when a ball is drawn <u>at random</u> from the machine containing the balls <u>1 to 49 inclusive</u>?

SHORTHAND NOTATION

1) $P(x) = 0.25$ simply means "the probability of event x happening is 0.25".
2) Eg: if you roll a dice, the <u>probability of rolling a 6</u> will be written as <u>P(rolls a 6)</u>.

Q3 After <u>49 tosses</u> of an unbiased coin, 24 have been heads and 25 have been tails. What is <u>P(50th toss will be a head)</u>?

Q4 If the probability of picking a banana from a fruit bowl is <u>0.27</u>, what is the probability of picking something which is <u>not</u> a banana?

Q5 A bag contains <u>3 red</u> balls, <u>4 blue</u> balls and <u>5 green</u> balls. A ball is chosen at random from the bag. What is the probability that:
a) it is green
b) it is blue
c) it is red
d) it is <u>not</u> red?

Q6 Students at school conduct a survey of the <u>colours</u> of parents' cars, where every parent owns one car. The table shows the results.

Red	Blue	Yellow	White	Green	Other
40	29	13	20	16	14

a) What is the probability of a parent owning a <u>red</u> car?
b) What is the probability of a parent owning a car that is <u>not</u> blue <u>or</u> green?

Q7 The probability of it raining during the monsoon is ¾, on a particular day.
a) What is the probability of it <u>not raining</u>?
b) If a monsoon 'season' lasts approximately <u>100 days</u>, how many days are likely to be <u>dry</u>?

Probability

Q8 Charlton's cricket team had the following results over their last 20 matches.

```
W W L D D W W L W L
D L L D W D W W L L
```

a) Complete the frequency table.

b) Charlton reasons that since there are 3 possible results for any match, the probability that the next match will be drawn (D) is $\frac{1}{3}$. Explain why Charlton is wrong.

Outcome	Frequency
W	
D	
L	

c) Suggest a value for the probability of a draw based on the past performance of Charlton's team.

Q9 a) What is the probability of randomly selecting either a black Ace or black King from an ordinary pack of playing cards?

Remember the OR rule — P(A or B) = P(A) + P(B).

b) If the entire suit of clubs is removed from a pack of cards, what is the probability of randomly selecting a red 7 from the remaining cards?

c) If all the 7s are also removed from the pack of cards, what is the probability of randomly selecting the 4 of diamonds?

Q10 For the roulette wheel shown, the probability of the ball landing on each of the numbers is listed in the table below.

Number	1	2	3	4	5	6
Probability	$\frac{1}{6}$	$\frac{1}{3}$	$\frac{1}{6}$	$\frac{1}{12}$	$\frac{1}{12}$	$\frac{1}{6}$

a) Find the probability of landing on an even number.
b) What is the probability of landing on black?
c) Why is the probability of landing on a white or a 3 not $\frac{5}{12} + \frac{1}{6}$?

Q11 The notepad below shows orders for 4 different sorts of rice at a certain Indian restaurant. Based on this data, what is the probability that the next order of rice is:

a) for pilau rice?
b) for spicy mushroom or special fried rice?
c) not for boiled rice?

```
boiled          20
pilau           24
spicy mushroom  10
special fried    6
```

If you're asked to work out probabilities based on some data, it's a relative frequency question.

UNIT TWO

Probability

Q12 There are 2 spinners: one with 3 sides numbered 1, 2, 3, and the other with 7 sides numbered 1, 2, 3, 4, 5, 6, 7.

a) If both are spun together, list all the possible outcomes.

b) Complete the following table showing the sum of the 2 numbers for each outcome.

	1	2	3	4	5	6	7
1							
2							
3							

c) What is the probability that the sum is 6?
d) What is the probability that the sum is even?
e) What is the probability that the sum is greater than or equal to 8?
f) What is the probability that the sum is less than 8?
g) Explain how you can work out the probability in part **f)** without using the table.

Q13 3 balls are drawn at random, without replacement, from a bag containing 4 green balls and 3 red balls.

a) Complete the tree diagram below showing all the possible outcomes and their probabilities.

For AND you MULTIPLY along the branches.
For OR you ADD the end results.

b) What is the probability that exactly 2 green balls are drawn?
c) What is the probability that the last ball drawn is the same colour as the first?

Probability

Q14 How many times must you roll an ordinary 6-sided dice for the probability of getting at least one 6 to be more than 0.5?

*Don't forget the "at least" trick —
P(at least 1 six) = 1 − P(no sixes).*

Q15 An unbiased dice in the shape of a tetrahedron has vertices numbered 1, 2, 3, 4. To win a game with this dice, you must throw a 4. At each go you have a maximum of 3 attempts.
a) Using a tree diagram, calculate the probability of winning with the second throw of the first go.
b) What is the probability of winning on the first go?

Q16 3 coins are drawn at random, without replacement, from a piggy bank containing 7 pound coins and 4 twenty-pence pieces.
a) Draw a tree diagram showing all possible outcomes and their probabilities.
b) Find the probability that the first coin selected is different in value from the third.
c) Find the probability that less than £1.50 is drawn altogether.

Q17 Fabrizio is practising taking penalties. The probability that he misses the goal completely is $\frac{1}{8}$. The probability that the goalkeeper saves the penalty is $\frac{3}{8}$. The probability that he scores is $\frac{1}{2}$. Fabrizio takes two penalties.
a) Calculate the probability that Fabrizio fails to score with his two penalties.
b) Calculate the probability that he scores only one goal.
c) Calculate the probability that Fabrizio scores on neither or both of his 2 attempts.

Q18 Trevor and his 2 brothers and 5 friends are seated at random in a row of 8 seats at the cinema. What is the probability that Trevor has one brother on his immediate left and one on his immediate right?

Careful here — you have to include the probability that Trevor sits in one of the six middle seats.

Drawing a tree diagram might be a bit of a faff, but it can really help to make the question clearer. So if you're stuck, give the old tree diagram a try.

UNIT TWO

Mean, Median, Mode, Range

For finding the <u>mode</u> and <u>median</u> put the data in order of size — it's much easier to find the most frequent and middle values.

The <u>mean</u> involves a bit more calculation, but hey, you're doing maths...

Q1 The local rugby team scored the following number of tries in their first 10 matches of the season:

| 3 | 5 | 4 | 2 | 0 | 1 | 3 | 0 | 3 | 4 |

Find their modal number of tries.

Q2 Find the mean, median, mode and range of these numbers:

| 1 | 2 | −2 | 0 | 1 | 8 | 3 | −3 | 2 | 4 | −2 | 2 |

Q3 A small company has 9 employees. Their salaries are as follows:

£13,000	£9,000	£7,500
£18,000	£12,000	£7,500
£23,000	£15,000	£11,500

a) Find the mean, median and mode of their salaries.
b) Which one does not give a good indication of their average salary?

Q4 Over a 3-week period, Molly kept a record of how many minutes her school bus was either early or late. (She used + for late and − for early.)

| +2 | −1 | 0 | +5 | −4 | −7 | 0 |
| −8 | 0 | +4 | −4 | −3 | +14 | +2 |

a) Calculate the mean lateness/earliness of the bus.
b) Calculate the median.
c) What is the mode?
d) The bus company use the answers to a), b) and c) to claim they are always on time. Is this true?

Careful with this — you have to use the averages to find the total weight, then divide to find the new average.

Q5 The average weight of the 11 players in a football team was 72.5 kg. The average weight of the 5 reserve players was 75.6 kg. What was the average weight of the whole squad? (Give your answer to 3 s.f.)

Q6 The mean daily weight of potatoes sold in a greengrocer's from Monday to Friday was 14 kg. The mean daily weight of potatoes sold from Monday to Saturday was 15 kg. How many kg of potatoes were sold on Saturday?

UNIT TWO

Mean, Median, Mode, Range

Q7 Colin averaged 83% over 3 exams. His average for the first two exams was 76%. What was Colin's score in the final exam?

Q8 The range for a certain list of numbers is 26, one of the numbers in the list is 48.
  a) What is the lowest possible value a number in the list could be?
  b) What is the highest possible value that could be in the list?

Q9 An ordinary dice is rolled 6 times, landing on a different number each time.
  a) What is the mean score?
  b) What is the median score?
  c) What is the range of scores?

Q10 The bar graph shows the amount of time Jim and Bob spend watching TV during the week.
  a) Find the mean amount of time per day each spends watching TV.
  b) Find the range of times for each of them.
  c) Using your answers from **a)** and **b)**, comment on what you notice about the way they watch TV.

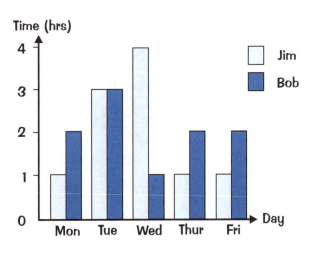

Q11 Mr Jones posted 88 Christmas cards first class on Monday. His friends received them over the week: 40 on Tuesday, 28 on Wednesday, 9 on Thursday, 6 on Friday and the remainder on Saturday.
  a) Find the modal number of days it took for the cards to arrive.
  b) Find the median number of days it took for the cards to arrive.
  c) "The majority of first class post arrives within 2 days." Is the above statement true or false in the light of the data?

Q12 In each of the following cases, decide which average is referred to:
  a) this average is least appropriate when the total number of values is small
  b) this average is least affected if one of the values is removed at random
  c) this average is most affected by the presence of extreme values.

UNIT TWO

Frequency Tables

You've got to be able to do these in both row and column form, because they could give you either one. There's no real difference, and the rules are still the same.

Q1 A travel company logs all calls to their sales desk. The number of calls per day received by the sales desk over a given year are shown below.

No. of Calls	10	11	12	13	14	15	16 and over
No. of Days	110	70	120	27	18	12	8

a) Find the median number of calls.
b) Find the modal number of calls.

Q2 A student has classes in Mathematics (M), English (E), French (F), Art (A) and Science (S). Her timetable is shown opposite.

Monday	S S E E A
Tuesday	E M M A A
Wednesday	S M E F F
Thursday	F E E A S
Friday	M M E S S

a) Complete the following frequency table for a week's lessons:

Subject	M	E	F	A	S
Frequency					

b) Calculate the number of French lessons that the student will attend during a 12-week term.

c) What is the modal lesson?

Q3 20 pupils are asked to estimate the length (to the nearest m) of their gardens.
Here are the results: 10, 8, 6, 4, 10, 8, 0, 14, 12, 8, 10, 6, 1, 6, 10, 8, 6, 6, 8, 8
Copy the frequency table below and put the estimates in.

a) Find the mode of the data.
b) Find the median of the data.
c) State the range of the data.

Length (m)	4 and under	6	8	10	12	14 and over
Frequency						

UNIT TWO

Frequency Tables

Q4 130 female bus drivers were weighed to the nearest kg.
Calculate:
a) the median weight
b) the modal weight
c) the mean weight, by first completing the table.

Weight (kg)	Frequency	Weight × Frequency
51	40	
52	30	
53	45	
54	10	
55	5	

Q5 A survey is carried out in a small village to find out how many bedrooms the houses have. The frequency table displays the results.

No. of bedrooms	1	2	3	4	5
Frequency	3	5	6	2	4

Find the mean, mode and median of the data.

Q6 A tornado has struck the hamlet of Moose-on-the-Wold. Many houses have had windows broken. The frequency table shows the devastating effects.

No. of windows broken per house	0	1	2	3	4	5	6
Frequency	5	3	4	11	13	7	2

a) Calculate the modal number of broken windows.
b) Calculate the median number of broken windows.
c) Calculate the mean number of broken windows.

Q7 Using the computerised till in a shoe shop, the manager can predict what stock to order from the previous week's sales.
Opposite is the tabularised printout for <u>last week</u> for <u>men's shoes</u>.

Shoe size	5	6	7	8	9	10	11
frequency	9	28	56	70	56	28	9

a) The mean, mode and median for this data can be compared. For each of the following statements decide whether it is true or false.
  i) The <u>mode</u> for this data is <u>70</u>.
  ii) The <u>mean</u> is <u>greater than</u> the <u>median</u> for this distribution.
  iii) The mean, median and mode are <u>all equal</u> in this distribution.

b) What <u>percentage</u> of customers bought shoes of the <u>mean size</u> from last week's sales data:

  i) 30% ii) 70% iii) 0.273% or iv) 27.3%?

UNIT TWO

Grouped Frequency

Q1 The speeds of 32 skiers at a certain corner of a downhill course are tabulated below.

Speed (km/h)	40 ≤ s < 45	45 ≤ s < 50	50 ≤ s < 55	55 ≤ s < 60	60 ≤ s < 65
Frequency	4	8	10	7	3
Mid-Interval					
Frequency × Mid-Interval					

a) By completing the frequency table, estimate the mean speed.
b) How many skiers were travelling at less than 55 km/h?
c) How many skiers were travelling at 50 km/h or faster?

Q2 The weights in kg of 18 newly felled trees are noted below:

272.7	333.2	251.0	246.5	328.0	259.6	200.2	312.8
344.3	226.8	362.0	348.3	256.1	232.9	309.7	398.0
284.5	327.4						

a) Complete the frequency table.

Weight (kg)	Tally	Frequency	Mid-Interval	Frequency × Mid-Interval
200 ≤ w < 250				
250 ≤ w < 300				
300 ≤ w < 350				
350 ≤ w < 400				

b) Estimate the mean weight using the frequency table.
c) What is the modal group?

Q3 48 numbers are recorded below:

0.057	0.805	0.056	0.979	0.419	0.160	0.534	0.763
0.642	0.569	0.773	0.055	0.349	0.892	0.664	0.136
0.528	0.792	0.085	0.546	0.549	0.908	0.639	0.000
0.614	0.478	0.421	0.472	0.292	0.579	0.542	0.356
0.070	0.890	0.883	0.333	0.033	0.323	0.544	0.668
0.094	0.049	0.049	0.999	0.632	0.700	0.983	0.356

a) Transfer the data into the frequency table.

Number	0 ≤ n < 0.2	0.2 ≤ n < 0.4	0.4 ≤ n < 0.6	0.6 ≤ n < 0.8	0.8 ≤ n < 1
Tally					
Frequency					
Mid-Interval					
Frequency × Mid-Interval					

b) Write down the modal class(es).
c) Which group contains the median?
d) Estimate the mean value.

UNIT TWO

Cumulative Frequency

Q1 Using the cumulative frequency curve, read off the:
a) median
b) lower quartile
c) upper quartile
d) interquartile range.

Q2 The following box plot shows the ages in years of trees in a wood.

a) What is the median age of the trees?
b) What is the upper quartile value?
c) What is the interquartile range?

Q3 The number of passengers using a bus service each day has been recorded over a 4-week period. The data is presented in the table below:

No. passengers	$0 \leq n < 50$	$50 \leq n < 100$	$100 \leq n < 150$	$150 \leq n < 200$	$200 \leq n < 250$	$250 \leq n < 300$
Frequency	2	7	10	5	3	1
Cumulative Frequency						
Mid-Interval						
Frequency × Mid-Interval						

A mean passenger

a) By completing the table, estimate the mean number of passengers.
b) By plotting a cumulative frequency curve, determine the median value.
c) What is the modal group?

With cumulative frequency you always plot the highest value from each class.

Q4 40 pupils have taken an exam and their marks are recorded in a frequency table.

Mark (%)	$0 \leq m < 20$	$20 \leq m < 40$	$40 \leq m < 60$	$60 \leq m < 80$	$80 \leq m < 100$
Frequency	2	12	18	5	3
Cumulative Frequency					

a) Complete the table and plot the cumulative frequency curve.
b) What is the value of the lower quartile?
c) What is the interquartile range?
d) What is the median mark?

UNIT TWO

Cumulative Frequency

Q5 One hundred scores for a board game are presented in the table below.

Score	$31 \leq s < 41$	$41 \leq s < 51$	$51 \leq s < 61$	$61 \leq s < 71$	$71 \leq s < 81$	$81 \leq s < 91$	$91 \leq s < 101$
Frequency	4	12	21	32	19	8	4
Cumulative Frequency							

a) What is the modal group?
b) Which group contains the median score?
c) By plotting the cumulative frequency curve determine the actual value of the median score.
d) Find the interquartile range.

Q6 The following frequency table gives the distribution of the lives of electric bulbs.

a) Complete the frequency table.

Life (hours)	Frequency	Cumulative Frequency
$900 \leq L < 1000$	10	
$1000 \leq L < 1100$	12	
$1100 \leq L < 1200$	15	
$1200 \leq L < 1300$	18	
$1300 \leq L < 1400$	22	
$1400 \leq L < 1500$	17	
$1500 \leq L < 1600$	14	
$1600 \leq L < 1700$	9	

b) Which group contains the median value?
c) By drawing the cumulative frequency curve, find the actual value of the median.
d) Determine values for the upper and lower quartiles.

Q7 30 pupils recorded the time taken (minutes : seconds) to boil some water.
Here are their results:
2:37 2:37 3:17 3:30 2:45 2:13 3:18 3:12 3:38 3:29
3:04 3:24 4:13 3:01 3:11 2:33 3:37 4:24 3:59 3:11
3:22 3:13 2:57 3:12 3:07 4:17 3:31 3:42 3:51 3:24

a) By using a tally, transfer the data into the frequency table.

Time	$2:00 \leq t < 2:30$	$2:30 \leq t < 3:00$	$3:00 \leq t < 3:30$	$3:30 \leq t < 4:00$	$4:00 \leq t < 4:30$
Tally					
Frequency					
Cumulative Frequency					

b) Draw the cumulative frequency curve.
c) Using your graph, read off the median and the upper and lower quartiles.
d) What is the interquartile range?

UNIT TWO

Histograms

It's the <u>size that counts</u>... You've got to look at the <u>area</u> of the bars to find the frequency. That means looking at the <u>width</u> as well as the height.

Q1 The histogram below represents the age distribution of people who watch outdoor bog snorkelling. Given that there are 24 people in the 40 – 55 age range, find the number of people in all the other age ranges.

You're given the frequency for one bar — use it to work out what each square represents.

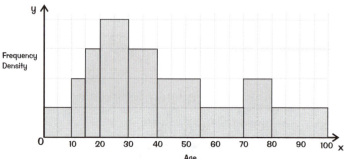

Q2 The weight of honey collected from several beehives is tabulated below.

a) Complete the frequency table by calculating the frequency densities.
b) Draw a histogram to represent this data.
c) Use your histogram to estimate the number of beehives that produced more than 6 kg of honey.

Weight (kg)	0 ≤ w < 2	2 ≤ w < 4	4 ≤ w < 7	7 ≤ w < 9	9 ≤ w < 15
Frequency	3	2	6	9	12
Frequency density					

Q3 Match the histograms to their corresponding cumulative frequency curves.

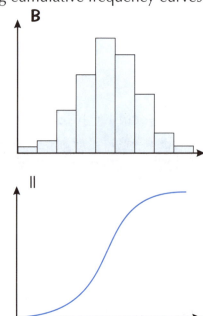

UNIT TWO

Histograms and Dispersion

 Know your shapes — they're bound to ask you what different-shaped graphs mean, so get learning.

Q1 A group of sixth formers took part in a survey to see how much time they spent watching TV each week.

a) Complete the table by filling in the frequency density column.
b) How many students took part in the survey?
c) Represent the data as a histogram.
d) Estimate the number of students that watch more than 7, but less than 13 hours each week.

No. of hours	Frequency	Frequency density
$0 \leq h < 1$	6	
$1 \leq h < 3$	13	
$3 \leq h < 5$	15	
$5 \leq h < 8$	9	
$8 \leq h < 10$	23	
$10 \leq h < 15$	25	
$15 \leq h < 20$	12	

Q2 Below are two histograms — one shows the weights of a sample of 16 year olds, and the other shows the weights of a sample of 1 kg bags of sugar. Say which is which.

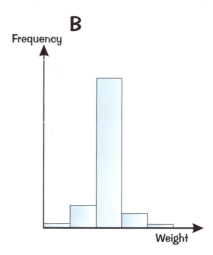

Q3 The lifetimes of 96 microwaves are tabulated:

Lifetime (years)	$0 \leq L < 2$	$2 \leq L < 4$	$4 \leq L < 6$	$6 \leq L < 8$	$8 \leq L < 10$	$10 \leq L < 12$
Frequency	15	22	36	9	10	4
Frequency density						
Mid-Interval						
Frequency × Mid-Interval						

a) Complete the frequency table.
b) Estimate the mean lifetime.
c) Which group contains the median value?
d) How many lifetimes are outside the modal group?
e) Draw a histogram and use it to determine the number of microwaves with lifetimes shorter than 5 years.

UNIT TWO

Histograms and Dispersion

Q4 A farmer keeps track of the amount of milk produced by his cows each day.

Amount of Milk (Litres)	Frequency	Frequency Density	Mid-Interval	Frequency × Mid-Interval
0 ≤ C < 1	6			
1 ≤ C < 5	6			
5 ≤ C < 8	6			
8 ≤ C < 10	6			
10 ≤ C < 15	6			
15 ≤ C < 20	6			

a) Complete the frequency table.
b) Use the mid-interval technique to estimate the mean.
c) Draw a histogram to show the data.
d) On how many days is less than 8 litres produced?

Q5 A magazine has carried out a survey to see how much pocket money its readers receive each week.

Amount (£)	Frequency	Frequency Density	Mid-Interval	Frequency × Mid-Interval
0 ≤ A < 0.50	11			
0.50 ≤ A < 1.00	25			
1.00 ≤ A < 1.30	9			
1.30 ≤ A < 1.50	12			
1.50 ≤ A < 1.80	24			
1.80 ≤ A < 2.50	21			
2.50 ≤ A < 3.10	54			
3.10 ≤ A < 4.10	32			

a) By first completing the table, estimate the mean amount of pocket money.
b) What is the modal class?
c) Draw a histogram to represent the data.
d) How many readers receive more than £1.40 each week?

Unit Two

Scatter Graphs

A **SCATTER GRAPH** is just a load of points on a graph that <u>end up in a bit of a mess</u>, rather than in a nice line or curve. There's a fancy word to say how much of a mess they're in — it's **CORRELATION**.

Q1 Match the following diagrams with the most appropriate descriptive label.
Labels:
(P) Strong positive correlation (S) Moderate negative correlation
(Q) Exact negative correlation (T) Medium correlation
(R) Little or no correlation (U) Exact positive correlation.

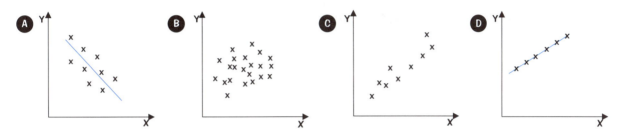

Q2 8 friends are comparing heights and shoe sizes to see if they are correlated.
The data is tabulated below:

Height	4'6"	4'8"	5'2"	5'5"	5'8"	5'10"	6'	6'6"
Shoe size	4	5	4.5	5	6	8	9	12

a) Plot the points on a scatter graph.
b) Are the points positively or negatively correlated?
c) By fitting an appropriate line, estimate the shoe size of another friend who is 6'2".

Q3 Janine is convinced that the more expensive cookery books contain more pages.
To test out her theory, she has compiled this table:

Price	£4.25	£5.00	£4.75	£6.25	£7.50	£8.25	£4.75	£5.00	£6.75	£3.25	£3.75
No. of pages	172	202	118	184	278	328	158	138	268	84	98

a) Draw a scatter graph to represent this information.
b) Draw in a line of best fit.
c) Use your line to estimate the price of a book containing 250 pages.

Q4 A local electrical store has kept a log of the number of CD players sold at each price:

Price (£)	£80	£150	£230	£310	£380	£460
No. Sold	27	24	22	19	17	15

a) Draw this information as a scatter graph, using suitable axes.
b) Draw a line of best fit and use it to estimate:
  i) the number of CD players the shopkeeper could expect to sell for £280
  ii) how much the shopkeeper should charge if he wanted to sell exactly 25 CD players.
c) Is the data positively or negatively correlated?

UNIT TWO

Pie Charts

Everyone loves a pie chart. Oh, no, sorry, that's pies...

When constructing a pie chart, follow the three steps:

1) Add up the numbers in each sector to get the TOTAL.
2) Divide 360° by the TOTAL to get the MULTIPLIER.
3) Multiply EVERY number by the MULTIPLIER to get the ANGLE of each SECTOR.

Q1 Construct a pie chart, using the template on the right, to show the following data:

Type of washing powder	Households on one estate using it
Swash	22
Sudso	17
Bubblefoam	18
Cleanyo	21
Wundersuds	12

Q2 In the year 1998/99, 380,000 students studied IT in Scotland. The distribution of students for the whole of Britain is shown in the pie chart.
Use a protractor on the diagram to find the number of students studying IT in each of the other parts of the U.K. (rounded to the nearest 10,000).

Use the info you're given to find the number of students represented by 1°.

The distribution of IT students throughout Britain

Q3 The pie chart shows the results of a survey of forty 11 year olds when asked what their favourite vegetable is with Sunday lunch. Which one of the following may be deduced from the information in the pie chart?

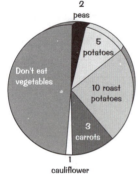

2 peas
5 potatoes
Don't eat vegetables
10 roast potatoes
3 carrots
1 cauliflower

a) Potatoes are the least popular vegetable.
b) 3/4 of the children like potatoes of some type.
c) 1/10 of the children like carrots or cauliflower.
d) 11/40 of the children asked what their favourite vegetable is, replied "Don't eat vegetables."

Q4 Mr and Mrs Tight think they have the family budget under control.
Mr and Mrs Spendthrift try to argue with Mr and Mrs Tight that they too can control their spending.
They produce two pie charts to represent their spending habits.
Give 2 reasons why these pie charts are unhelpful.

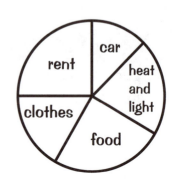

UNIT TWO

Sampling Methods

Q1 Define:
  a) random sampling
  b) systematic sampling
  c) stratified sampling

You've got to know the main types of sampling — make sure you can answer Q1 before going on to the rest.

You've also got to be able to spot problems and criticise sampling techniques — basically, if you think it's a load of rubbish, you get the chance to say why.

Q2 Give a reason why the following methods of sampling are poor:
  a) a survey carried out inside a newsagents concluded that 80% of the population buy a daily newspaper
  b) a phone poll conducted at 11 am on a Sunday morning revealed that less than 2% of the population regularly go to church
  c) 60% of the population were estimated to watch the 9 o'clock news each evening after a survey was carried out at a bridge club.

Q3 Decide which of the following questions (if any) are suitable for a survey to find which of five desserts (cheesecake, fruit salad, sherry trifle, knickerbocker glory and chocolate cake) people like the most. Give a reason for each of your answers.
  a) Do you like cheesecake, fruit salad, sherry trifle, knickerbocker glory or chocolate cake?
  b) How often do you eat dessert?
  c) Which is your favourite out of: cheesecake; fruit salad; sherry trifle; knickerbocker glory; chocolate cake?
  d) What is your favourite dessert?
  e) Is your favourite dessert: cheesecake; fruit salad; sherry trifle; knickerbocker glory; chocolate cake; none of these?

Q4 A newspaper contained the following article regarding the amount of exercise teenagers take outside school.

  a) Suggest 3 questions that you could use in a survey to find out whether this is true at your school.
  b) At a particular school there are 300 pupils in each of years 7 to 11. There are approximately equal numbers of girls and boys.
  Describe how you would select 10% of the pupils for a stratified sample which is representative of all the pupils at the school.

Over half of all teenagers do no exercise at all. Only one in ten play team sports or take part in individual sports.

UNIT TWO

Sampling Methods

Q5 Pauline is the manager of a small café. She knows that some of her customers buy cold drinks from the cold drinks machine, some buy hot drinks from the hot drinks machine and some people buy snacks and drinks at the counter.

Pauline would like to use a questionnaire to find out whether she should stock a new brand of cola. Here is part of Pauline's questionnaire:

Café Questionnaire

1) Please tick the box to show how often you visit the café:

daily ☐   weekly ☐   fortnightly ☐   monthly ☐   less than monthly ☐

a) Using the same style, design another question that Pauline can include in her questionnaire.

b) Pauline hands out her questionnaire as she serves customers at the counter. Give a reason why this is a suitable or unsuitable way to hand out the questionnaire.

Statistics Crossword

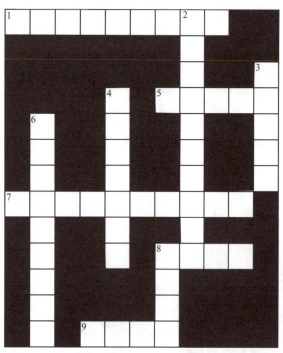

ACROSS
1) You can easily find the range and average from this type of table. (9)
5) A method of sampling which tries to use the same proportions as the whole population. (5)
7) There's more than one layer to this sort of sampling. (10)
8) It's not a matter of being cruel, its just a way of working out averages. (4)
9) With so many choices no wonder these diagrams branch off in so many directions. (4)

DOWN
2) Adding it up as you go along. (10)
3) Distance from the lowest to highest. (5)
4) This graph is more scat. (7)
6) It's not the height but the area of each bar that matters with this type of chart. (9)
8) Perhaps the most common way of finding an average. (4)

Time Series

 Two important things you need to spot with time series — trends and seasonality. A trend is the overall change in the data. Watch out for a repeating pattern — it means the series is seasonal.

Q1 Which of the following sets of measurements form time series?
  a) The average rainfall in Cumbria, measured each day for a year.
  b) The daily rainfall in European capital cities on Christmas Day, 2000.
  c) The shoe size of everybody in Class 6C on September 1st, 2001.
  d) My shoe size (measured every month) from when I was twelve months old to when I was fourteen years old.

Q2 a) Which two of the following time series are seasonal, and which two are not seasonal?

  b) What are the periods of the time series which are seasonal?
  c) Describe the trends in the time series which are **not** seasonal.

Q3 The following table shows the value of a knitwear company's sock sales in the years 1998-2000. The sales figures are given in thousands of pounds.

Time	Sales
Spring 1998	404
Summer 1998	401
Autumn 1998	411
Winter 1998	420
Spring 1999	416
Summer 1999	409
Autumn 1999	419
Winter 1999	424
Spring 2000	416
Summer 2000	413
Autumn 2000	427
Winter 2000	440

  a) Plot the figures on a graph with time on the horizontal axis and sales on the vertical axis.
  b) Calculate a 4-point moving average to smooth the series. Copy the table and write your answers in the empty boxes.
  c) Plot the moving average on the same axes as your original graph.
  d) Describe the trend of the sales figures.

Unit Two

UNIT THREE

Types of Number

There are a few special number sequences that you really need to know — SQUARE, CUBE, TRIANGULAR and PRIME NUMBERS, as well as POWERS and ODD and EVEN NUMBERS.

Q1 Sarah thinks of a number. She calculates that the square of the number is 256. What is the square root of the number?

Q2 On a certain day the temperature at midday was 14°C. By midnight the temperature had fallen by 17°C. What was the temperature at midnight?

Q3 The number one is the first odd number. It is also the first square number, the first cube number and the first triangle number.
  a) Which is greater: the third odd number, the third square number or the third cube number?
  b) Write down the prime factors of the third triangle number.

Q4 The following sequences are described in words. Write down their first four terms.
  a) The prime numbers starting from 17.
  b) The squares of odd numbers starting from $9^2=81$.
  c) The triangular numbers starting from 15.

Q5 Using any or all of the figures **1, 2, 5, 9** write down:
  a) the smallest prime number
  b) a prime number greater than 20
  c) a prime number between 10 and 20
  d) two prime numbers whose sum is 21
  e) a number that is not prime.

Remember — 1 is not a prime. Look, it just isn't, OK.

Q6 a) In the ten by ten square opposite, ring all the <u>prime numbers</u>. (The first three have been done for you.)
  b) Among the prime numbers between 10 and 100, find three which are still prime when their digits are reversed.
  c) Give a reason for 27 not being a prime number.

1	②	③	4	⑤	6	7	8	9	10
11	12	13	14	15	16	17	18	19	20
21	22	23	24	25	26	27	28	29	30
31	32	33	34	35	36	37	38	39	40
41	42	43	44	45	46	47	48	49	50
51	52	53	54	55	56	57	58	59	60
61	62	63	64	65	66	67	68	69	70
71	72	73	74	75	76	77	78	79	80
81	82	83	84	85	86	87	88	89	90
91	92	93	94	95	96	97	98	99	100

Q7 What is the largest prime less than 300?

Q8 How many prime numbers are even?

Multiples, Factors and Primes

Q1 1   3   6   9   12
From the numbers above, write down:
a) a multiple of 4
b) the prime number
c) two square numbers
d) three factors of 27
e) two numbers P and Q that satisfy both P=2Q and P=$\sqrt{144}$

This is real basic stuff — you just have to know your times tables. And your primes, of course...

Q2 A school ran 3 evening classes: Conversational French, Cake Making and Woodturning. The Conversational French class had 29 students, Cake Making had 27 students, and the Woodturning class had 23. For which classes did the teacher have difficulty dividing the students into equal groups?

Q3
a) Find the lowest common multiple of 5 and 9.
b) Find the lowest common multiple of 4 and 6.
c) Find the lowest common multiple of 4, 6 and 8.
d) Find the highest common factor of 26 and 52.
e) Find the highest common factor of 26, 39 and 52.

Q4
a) Write down the first five cube numbers.
b) Which of the numbers given in part **a)** are multiples of 2?
c) Which of the numbers given in part **a)** are multiples of 3?
d) Which of the numbers given in part **a)** are multiples of 4?
e) Which of the numbers given in part **a)** are multiples of 5?

Q5 Express the following as a product of prime factors:
a) 18
b) 140
c) 47

The tricky bit is remembering that a <u>prime factorisation</u> includes <u>all</u> the prime factors that multiply to make that number — so you've got to repeat some of them.

Q6
a) List the first five prime numbers.
b) If added together, what is their total?
c) Write down the prime factorisation of the answer to part **b)**.

Q7
a) List the first five odd numbers.
b) If added together, what is their total?
c) Write down the prime factorisation of the answer to part **b)**.

Unit Three

Multiples, Factors and Primes

Q8   The prime factorisation of a certain number is $3^2 \times 5 \times 11$.
   a) Write down the number.
   b) Write down the prime factorisation of 165.

Q9   **a)** Write down the first ten triangle numbers.
   b) From your list pick out all multiples of 2.
   c) From your list pick out all multiples of 3.
   d) From your list pick out any prime numbers.
   e) Add the numbers in your list together and write down the prime factorisation of the total.

Q10   Gordon is doing some woodwork and needs to calculate the volume of a wooden rectangular block (cuboid).
   The length of the block is 50 cm, the height 25 cm and the width 16 cm.
   a) What is the volume (in cm^3) of the wooden block?
   b) What is the prime factorisation of the number found in part **a)**?

   Gordon needs to cut the block into smaller blocks with dimensions 4 cm × 5 cm × 5 cm.
   c) What is the maximum number of small blocks Gordon can make from the larger block? Make sure you show all your working.

Q11   The prime factorisation of a certain number is $2^3 \times 5 \times 17$.
   a) What is the number?
   b) What is the prime factorisation of half of this number?
   c) What is the prime factorisation of a quarter of the number?
   d) What is the prime factorisation of an eighth of the number?

Q12   Bryan and Sue were playing a guessing game. Sue thought of a number between 1 and 100 which Bryan had to guess. Bryan was allowed to ask five questions, which are listed with Sue's responses in the table below.

Bryan's Questions	Sue's Responses
Is it prime?	No
Is it odd?	No
Is it less than 50?	Yes
Is it a multiple of 3?	Yes
Is it a multiple of 7?	Yes

Start by writing down a number table up to 100. Look at each response in turn and cross off numbers 'till you've only got one left.

What is the number that Sue thought of?

UNIT THREE

Fractions and Decimals

Decimals are just another way of writing fractions —
so it's easy to convert between the two...

Q1 Without using a calculator, write the following fractions as decimals:

a) $\dfrac{3}{10}$ b) $\dfrac{37}{100}$ c) $\dfrac{2}{5}$ d) $\dfrac{3}{8}$

Q2 Write the following fractions as recurring decimals:

a) $\dfrac{5}{6}$ b) $\dfrac{7}{9}$ c) $\dfrac{7}{11}$ d) $\dfrac{47}{99}$

Q3 Fill in the gaps in the following conversion table:

Fraction	Decimal
½	0.5
⅕	
	0.125
	1.6
4⁄16	
7⁄2	
	0.x
x⁄100	
3⁄20	
	0.45

Q4 Write the following decimals as fractions in their lowest form:

a) 0.6   b) 0.75   c) 0.95   d) 0.128

Q5 Write the following recurring decimals as fractions in their lowest form:

a) 0.222...   b) 0.444...   c) 0.888...   d) 0.808080...

e) 0.121212...   f) 0.545545545...   g) 0.753753753...   h) 0.156156156...

Q6 Do the following without a calculator, giving your answer as a fraction in its lowest terms:

a) $\dfrac{1}{2}+\dfrac{1}{4}$ e) $6\times\dfrac{2}{3}$ i) $3+\dfrac{8}{5}$

b) $\dfrac{2}{3}-\dfrac{1}{4}$ f) $\dfrac{4}{5}\div\dfrac{2}{3}$ j) $\dfrac{2}{3}\left(\dfrac{3}{4}+\dfrac{4}{5}\right)$

c) $\dfrac{1}{5}+\dfrac{2}{3}-\dfrac{2}{5}$ g) $\dfrac{5}{12}\times\dfrac{3}{2}$ k) $\left(\dfrac{1}{7}+\dfrac{3}{14}\right)\times\left(3-\dfrac{1}{5}\right)$

d) $5-\dfrac{1}{4}$ h) $\dfrac{5}{6}-\dfrac{7}{8}$ l) $\left(\dfrac{3}{4}-\dfrac{1}{5}\right)\div\left(\dfrac{7}{8}+\dfrac{1}{16}\right)$

Unit Three

Sequences

Q1 For each of the sequences below, write down the next three numbers and the rule that you used.

    a) 1, 3, 5, 7,...

    b) 2, 4, 8, 16,...

    c) 3, 30, 300, 3000,...

    d) 3, 7, 11, 15,...

    e) 19, 14, 9, 4, –1,...

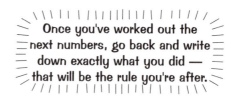
Once you've worked out the next numbers, go back and write down exactly what you did — that will be the rule you're after.

Q2 In the following, use the rule given to generate the first 5 terms of the sequence.

    a) $3n + 1$, when $n = 1, 2, 3, 4$ and 5.

    b) $5n - 2$, when $n = 1, 2, 3, 4$ and 5.

    c) n^2, when $n = 1, 2, 3, 4,$ and 5.

    d) $n^2 - 3$, when $n = 1, 2, 3, 4,$ and 5.

Q3 Write down an expression for the nth term of the following sequences:

    a) 2, 4, 6, 8, ...

    b) 1, 3, 5, 7, ...

    c) 5, 10, 15, 20, ...

    d) 5, 8, 11, 14, ...

Q4 In the following sequences, write down the next 3 terms and the *n*th term:

    a) 7, 10, 13, 16,...   **c)** 6, 16, 26, 36,...

    b) 12, 17, 22, 27,...   **d)** 54, 61, 68, 75,...

UNIT THREE

Sequences

Q5 10, 20, 15, 17½, 16¼...
a) Write down the next 4 terms.
b) Explain how you would work out the 10th term.

Q6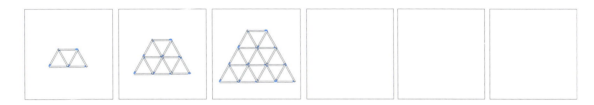

The pattern above is based on individual triangles.
a) Write down the number of individual triangles in each group shown above.
b) Work out the number of individual triangles that would be in each of the next three groups.
c) Find a formula for the number of individual triangles in the nth term of the pattern.

For the increasing/decreasing difference type questions you've got to work out how much the difference changes by each time.

Q7 Write down the next three terms and nth term of:

a) 5, 8, 12, 17,...
b) 6, 9, 14, 21,...
c) 9, 12, 19, 30,...
d) 14, 19, 27, 38,...

e) 729, 243, 81, 27,...
f) 31250, 6250, 1250, 250,...
g) 12288, 3072, 768, 192,...
h) 5103, 1701, 567, 189,...

Q8 A square tile pattern is formed with grey and white tiles. In the centre there is always a grey tile. The rest of the pattern is made up of alternating grey and white tiles, with the four corner tiles of the square always being grey.
Assume that $n = 1$ in the pattern shown opposite.

Work out, in terms of n, the formula for:
a) the number of grey tiles
b) the number of white tiles
c) the total number of tiles.

Calculator Buttons

Q1 Using the $\boxed{x^2}$ button on your calculator, work out:

a) 1^2 **d)** 16^2 **g)** $(-5)^2$

b) 2^2 **e)** $(-1)^2$ **h)** 1000^2

c) 11^2 **f)** 30^2 **i)** 0^2

Q2 Using the $\boxed{\sqrt{}}$ button on your calculator, work out:

a) $\sqrt{16}$ **d)** $\sqrt{0}$ **g)** $\sqrt{3}$

b) $\sqrt{36}$ **e)** $\sqrt{3600}$ **h)** $\sqrt{7}$

c) $\sqrt{289}$ **f)** $\sqrt{400}$ **i)** $\sqrt{30}$

Q3 Use the $\boxed{\sqrt[3]{}}$ button on your calculator to work out:

a) $\sqrt[3]{1}$ **e)** $\sqrt[3]{27}$

b) $\sqrt[3]{0}$ **f)** $\sqrt[3]{-27}$

c) $\sqrt[3]{343}$ **g)** $\sqrt[3]{-64}$

d) $\sqrt[3]{1000}$ **h)** $\sqrt[3]{-5}$

> Yeah, OK, we all know how to do sums on a calculator — but it can do so much more... check out the groovy powers button and the funky brackets buttons, not to mention the slinky $\boxed{1/x}$ button...

Q4 By calculating the bottom line (the denominator) first and storing it in your calculator, work out:

a) $\dfrac{21}{2+\sin 30°}$ **c)** $\dfrac{15}{\cos 30° + 22}$ **e)** $\dfrac{12}{12+\tan 60°}$

b) $\dfrac{\tan 15°}{12+12^2}$ **d)** $\dfrac{18}{3+\sqrt[3]{12}}$ **f)** $\dfrac{18}{11+\tan 77°}$

Q5 Using $\boxed{[(\text{---}}$ and $\boxed{\text{---})]}$, calculate:

> Here comes BODMAS...

a) $\dfrac{(14+18)}{(2\times 8)}$ **c)** $\dfrac{(9+(4\div 2))}{(11\times 3)}$ **e)** $\dfrac{12}{(8+9)(13-11)}$

b) $\dfrac{8}{(1\times 4)(8-6)}$ **d)** $\dfrac{14(4\times 8)}{(6+9)}$ **f)** $\dfrac{7(5+4)}{12(9\times 8)}$

Q6 Using the $\boxed{x^y}$ or $\boxed{\wedge}$ button, find:

a) 2^0 **d)** π^2 **g)** $(\cos 30°)^5$

b) 4^{10} **e)** 2^{-1} **h)** 4.29^7

c) 2^{20} **f)** 3^{10} **i)** $(\sin 45°)^4$

UNIT THREE

Conversion Factors and Metric & Imperial Units

You've got to know all the metric and imperial conversion factors — there's no way out of it, you'll just have to sit down and learn them, sorry and all that...

Q1 Express the given quantity in the unit(s) in brackets:

a) 2 m [cm] **g)** 87 in [ft and in] **m)** 6 ft [in] **s)** 8 cm 6 mm [mm]

b) 3.3 cm [mm] **h)** 43 oz [lb and oz] **n)** 5 lb [oz] **t)** 3 ft 6 in [in]

c) 4 kg [g] **i)** 650 m [km] **o)** 301 ft [yd and ft] **u)** 4 lb 7 oz [oz]

d) 600 g [kg] **j)** 9 kg [g] **p)** 6 m [mm] **v)** 550 kg [tonnes]

e) 4 ft [in] **k)** 7 g [kg] **q)** 2 tonnes [kg] **w)** 3 m 54 cm [cm]

f) 36 in [ft] **l)** 950 g [kg] **r)** 3000 g [kg] **x)** 0.7 cm [mm]

Q2 Convert 147 kg into pounds.

Q3 Convert the following into hours and minutes:

a) 3.25 hours **b)** 0.4 hours **c)** 7.3 hours **d)** 1.2 hours.

Q4 A horse's drinking trough holds 14 gallons of water.
Approximately how many litres is this?

Q5 Deborah weighs 9 stone 4 pounds.
There are 14 pounds in a stone and 1 kilogram is equal to 0.157 stone.
Change Deborah's weight into kilograms.

Q6 A pile of bricks weighs 7 metric tonnes. Approximately how many imperial tons is this?

Q7 Barbara cycled 51 km in one day while Barry cycled 30 miles. Who cycled further?

Q8 A seamstress needs to cut an 11 inch strip of finest Chinese silk.
a) Approximately how many cm is this?
b) Approximately how many mm is this?

Q9 The priceless Greek statue in my garden is 21 feet tall.

a) How many inches is this? **d)** How many cm is this?

b) How many yards is this? **e)** How many mm is this?

c) How many metres is this? **f)** How many km is this?

Q10 A recipe for The World's Wobbliest Jelly requires 5 lb of sugar. How many 1 kg bags of sugar does Dick need to buy so that he can make a jelly?

Q11 The Bon Voyage Holiday Company are offering an exchange rate of 1.48 euros for £1 sterling. They are also offering 11.03 Danish kroner for £1 sterling and 2.45 Australian dollars for £1 sterling. Calculate, to the nearest penny, the sterling equivalent of:

a) 220 euros **g)** 899 Danish kroner

b) 686 Danish kroner **h)** 20 euros

c) 1664 Australian dollars **i)** 668 Australian dollars

d) 148 euros **j)** 3389 Danish kroner

e) 15 Danish kroner **k)** 1000 Australian dollars

f) 1950 Australian dollars **l)** 1 euro

UNIT THREE

Conversion Factors and Metric & Imperial Units

Q12 At the gym Arnold can lift a barbell weighing 60 kg.
a) Approximately how many lbs is this?
b) How many ounces is this?
Sylvester can lift a barbell weighing 0.059 tonnes.
c) Who can lift the most?

Q13 The scale on a map is 1:10 000.
How big are the following in real life:
a) a distance of 2 cm on the map
b) a distance of 20 cm on the map
c) a distance of 70 cm on the map
d) an area of 2 cm^2 on the map?

Maps can be tricky. Best thing is to keep the units the same when you do the initial conversion, then do another conversion to the appropriate units.

Q14 Another map has a scale of 1:3000.
What size on this map are the following:
a) a distance of 5 km in real life
b) a distance of 1 km in real life
c) an area of 100 m^2 in real life
d) an area of 50 m^2 in real life?

Just remember — the distance on the map is unlikely to be larger than the real-life distance.

Q15
```
1 pint = 0.568 litres
£1 = $1.42
```

Which is better value, 2 pints of beer for $5.76 or 1 litre of beer for £3.92?

Q16 Neil is going to buy some fabric for a new pair of trousers that he is going to make. A local shop prices the fabric that he would like at £9.84 per square yard. A fabric superstore prices the same fabric at £10.80 per square metre. According to price, where should Neil buy his fabric? (Use the conversion factor 91 cm = 1 yard.)

UNIT THREE

Rounding Off & Estimating

Rounding a number off to a certain number of decimal places or significant figures is really quite easy. Estimating is a bit trickier — you have to change the numbers into nice ones that you can deal with without using your calculator.

Q1 $K = 456.9873$
Write K correct to:

a) one decimal place
b) two decimal places
c) three decimal places
d) three significant figures
e) two significant figures
f) one significant figure.

Q2 Without using your calculator find approximate answers to the following:

a) 6560×1.97
b) 8091×1.456
c) $38.45 \times 1.4237 \times 5.0002$
d) $45.34 \div 9.345$
e) $34504 \div 7133$
f) $\dfrac{55.33 \times 19.345}{9.23}$
g) 7139×2.13
h) $98 \times 2.54 \times 2.033$
i) $21 \times 21 \times 21$
j) $8143 \div 81$
k) $62000 \div 950$
l) $\pi \div 3$

Q3 Estimate the area under the graph.

Q4 A supermarket chain sold 14 634 tins of beans during a four-week period.

a) If the supermarkets were open every day of the week, how many days did it take to sell the 14 634 tins of beans?
b) What was the average number of tins of beans sold each day?
c) Show your working for a rough estimate to **b)** to check that your answer is of the right order of magnitude.

"of the right order of magnitude" is just a posh way of saying "the right size", by the way.

Q5 π is the number of times that the diameter of a circle divides into the circumference. Many values have been used as estimates — here are a few examples:

$$3, \quad \frac{22}{7}, \quad \sqrt{10}, \quad \frac{255}{81}, \quad 3\frac{17}{120}.$$

a) Use your calculator to give each estimate correct to 7 decimal places.
b) Which is the most accurate estimate for π?

UNIT THREE

Speed

This is an easy enough formula — and of course you can put it in that good old formula triangle as well.

Average speed = Total distance / Total time

Q1 A train travels 240 km in 4 hours. What is its <u>average speed</u>?

Q2 A car travels for 3 hours at an average speed of 55 mph. How far has it travelled?

Q3 A boy rides a bike at an average speed of 15 km/h. How long will it take him to ride 40 km?

Q4 <u>Complete</u> this table.

Distance Travelled	Time taken	Average Speed
210 km	3 hrs	
135 miles		30 mph
	2 hrs 30 mins	42 km/h
9 miles	45 mins	
640 km		800 km/h
	1 hr 10 mins	60 mph

Q5 An athlete can run 100 m in 11 seconds.
Calculate the athlete's speed in:
a) m/s
b) km/h.

Q6 A plane flies over city A at 09.55 and over city B at 10.02. What is its <u>average</u> speed if these cities are 63 miles apart?

Q7 The distance from Kendal (Oxenholme) to London (Euston) is 280 miles. The train travels at an average speed of 63 mph. If I catch the 07.05 from Kendal, can I be at a meeting in London by 10.30? <u>Show all your working</u>.

Q8 In a speed trial a sand yacht travelled a measured mile in 36.4 seconds.
a) Calculate this speed in mph.
On the return mile he took 36.16 seconds.
b) Find his <u>total time</u> for the two runs.
c) Calculate the average speed of the two runs in mph.

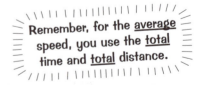

Remember, for the <u>average</u> speed, you use the <u>total</u> time and <u>total</u> distance.

Q9 A motorist drives from Manchester to London. 180 miles is on motorway where he averages 65 mph. 55 miles is on city roads where he averages 28 mph, 15 miles is on country roads where he averages 25 mph.
a) Calculate the total time taken for the journey.
b) How far did he travel altogether?
c) Calculate the average speed for the journey.

UNIT THREE

Density

Here we go again — the multi-purpose formula triangle. Learn the positions of M, D and V, plug in the numbers and pull out the answer... magic.

Q1 Find the density of each of these pieces of wood, giving your answer in g/cm³:
   a) Mass 3 g, volume 4 cm³
   b) Mass 12 kg, volume 20,000 cm³
   c) Mass 20 g, volume 25 cm³
   d) Mass 14 kg, volume 0.02 m³.

Q2 Calculate the mass of each of these objects:
   a) a small marble statue of density 2.6 g/cm³ and volume 24 cm³
   b) a plastic cube of volume 64 cm³ and density 1.5 g/cm³
   c) a gold ingot measuring 12 cm by 4 cm by 4 cm with density 19.5 g/cm³
   d) a pebble with volume 30 cm³ and density 2.5 g/cm³.

Q3 Work out the volume of each of these items:
   a) a bag of sugar of mass 1 kg and density 1.6 g/cm³
   b) a packet of margarine with density 2.8 g/cm³ and mass 250 g
   c) a 50 kg sack of coal with density 1.8 g/cm³
   d) a box of cereal with density 0.2 g/cm³ and mass 500 g.

Q4 My copper bracelet has a volume of 3.9 cm³. The density of copper is 8.9 g/cm³. Work out the mass of my bracelet.

Q5 Ice has a density of 0.93 g/cm³. If the mass of a block of ice is 19.5 kg, what is its volume?

Q6 Some petrol in a can has a mass of 4 kg. The density of the petrol is 0.8 g/cm³. How many litres of petrol are in the can?
1 litre = 1000 cm³.

Q7 A jug holds 1.9 litres of lemonade. The mass of the lemonade is 2 kg. Find the density of the lemonade.

Q8 A 1.5 kg bag full of self raising flour measures 12 cm by 18 cm by 6 cm. A 1 kg bag of granary flour measures 10 cm by 14 cm by 6 cm. Find the density of each sort of flour.

UNIT THREE

Powers and Roots

Hang on there. Before you try this page, make sure you know all the rules for dealing with powers...

The small number is called the **power** or **index number**. Remember the plural of index is **indices**.

To save time try using the power button on your calculator

Q1 Complete the following:
a) $2^4 = 2 \times 2 \times 2 \times 2 =$
b) $10^3 = 10 \times 10 \times 10 =$
c) $3^5 = 3 \times ... \quad =$
d) $4^6 = 4 \times \qquad =$
e) $1^9 = 1 \times \qquad =$
f) $5^6 = 5 \times \qquad =$

Q2 Simplify the following:
a) $2 \times 2 \times 2 \times 2 \times 2 \times 2 \times 2 \times 2$
b) $12 \times 12 \times 12 \times 12 \times 12$
c) $x \times x \times x \times x \times x \times x$
d) $m \times m \times m$
e) $y \times y \times y \times y$
f) $z \times z \times z \times z \times z \times z$

Q3 Complete the following (the first one has been done for you):
a) $10^2 \times 10^3 = (10 \times 10) \times (10 \times 10 \times 10) = 10^5$
b) $10^3 \times 10^4 = \qquad =$
c) $10^4 \times 10^2 = \qquad =$
d) $10^5 \times 10^3 = \qquad =$
e) What is the <u>quick method</u> for writing down the final result in **b)**, **c)** and **d)**?

Easy — you'll have learnt this from your power rules.

Q4 Complete the following (the first one has been done for you):
a) $2^4 \div 2^2 = \dfrac{(2 \times 2 \times 2 \times 2)}{(2 \times 2)} = 2^2$
b) $2^5 \div 2^2 = \dfrac{(2 \times 2 \times 2 \times 2 \times 2)}{(2 \times 2)} =$
c) $4^5 \div 4^3 = \dfrac{(4 \times 4 \times 4 \times 4 \times 4)}{} =$
d) $8^5 \div 8^2 = \qquad =$

e) What is the quick method for writing down the final result in **b)**, **c)** and **d)**?

Q5 Which of the following are <u>true</u>?
a) $2^4 \times 2^6 = 2^{10}$
b) $2^2 \times 2^3 \times 2^4 = 2^9$
c) $2^3 \times 2^2 = 2^6$
d) $4^{10} \times 4^4 \times 4^2 = 4^{18}$
e) $2^1 \times 2^3 \times 2^4 = 2^8$
f) $10^4 \times 10^2 = 10^8$
g) $2^{20} \div 2^5 = 2^4$
h) $3^{12} \div 3^4 = 3^8$
i) $4^6 \div 6^4 = 4^2$
j) $10^{20} \div 10^3 = 10^{17}$
k) $4^6 \div (4^2 \times 4^3) = 4^1$
l) $9^2 \times (9^{30} \div 9^{25}) = 9^{10}$

Q6 Remove the brackets from the following and express as a single power:
a) $(3^4 \times 3^2) \div (3^6 \times 3^3)$
b) $(4^{10} \times 4^{12}) \times 4^3$
c) $10^2 \div (10^3 \times 10^{12})$
d) $(3^6)^{-2}$
e) $4^2 \times 4^{-1} \times 4^6 \times (4^2 \div 4^3)$
f) $(5^2 \times 5^3) \div (5^6 \div 5^4)$

UNIT THREE

Powers and Roots

For Questions 7 to 11 answers should be given to 3 s.f. where necessary.

Q7
a) $(6.5)^3$
b) $(0.35)^2$
c) $(15.2)^4$
d) $(0.04)^3$
e) $\sqrt{5.6}$
f) $\sqrt[3]{12.4}$
g) $\sqrt{109}$
h) $\sqrt[3]{0.6}$
i) $(1\frac{1}{2})^2$
j) $\sqrt{4\frac{3}{4}}$
k) $\left(\frac{5}{8}\right)^3$
l) $\sqrt[3]{\frac{9}{10}}$

Q8
a) $(2.4)^2 + 3$
b) $5.9 - (1.2)^3$
c) $\sqrt[3]{5.6} + (4.2)^2$
d) $(6.05)^3 - \sqrt[3]{8.4}$
e) $6.1[35.4 - (4.2)^2]$
f) $95 - 3(\sqrt[3]{48} - 2.6)$
g) $1\frac{1}{2}[4 + (2\frac{1}{4})^2]$
h) $19 - 4[(\frac{1}{4})^2 + ((\frac{5}{8})^3)]$
i) $15\frac{3}{5} - 2\frac{1}{2}[(1\frac{3}{4})^3 - \sqrt[3]{1\frac{1}{2}}]$

Q9
a) 5^{-3}
b) 2^{-2}
c) 16^{-4}
d) $(1.5)^{-1}$
e) $5^{\frac{1}{2}}$
f) $6^{\frac{1}{3}}$
g) $9^{\frac{1}{5}}$
h) $(4.2)^{\frac{2}{3}}$
i) $(1\frac{1}{4})^{-3}$
j) $(2\frac{3}{5})^{\frac{1}{5}}$
k) $(5\frac{1}{3})^{-2}$
l) $(10\frac{5}{6})^{\frac{5}{6}}$

Remember — fractional powers mean roots.

Q10
a) $\sqrt{(1.4)^2 + (0.5)^2}$
b) $5.9\,[(2.3)^{\frac{1}{4}} + (4.7)^{\frac{1}{2}}]$
c) $2.5 - 0.6[(7.1)^{-3} - (9.5)^{-4}]$
d) $(8.2)^{-2} + (1.6)^4 - (3.7)^{-3}$
e) $\dfrac{3\sqrt{8} - 2}{6}$
f) $\dfrac{15 + 3\sqrt{4.1}}{2.4}$
g) $3\sqrt{4.7} - 4\sqrt{2.1}$
h) $\dfrac{(2\frac{1}{4})^{-2} - (3\frac{1}{2})^{\frac{1}{2}}}{4.4}$

Q11
a) $(2\frac{1}{4})^3 - (1.5)^2$
b) $(3.7)^{-2} + (4\frac{1}{5})^{\frac{1}{4}}$
c) $\sqrt[3]{5\frac{1}{3}} \times (4.3)^{-1}$
d) $(7.4)^{\frac{1}{3}} \times (6\frac{1}{4})^3$
e) $\dfrac{\sqrt{22\frac{1}{2}} + (3.4)^2}{(6.9)^3 \times 3.4}$
f) $\dfrac{(15\frac{3}{5})^2 \times (2.5)^{-3}}{3 \times 4\frac{1}{4}}$
g) $5[(4.3)^2 - (2.5)^{\frac{1}{2}}]$
h) $\dfrac{3.5(2\frac{1}{6} - \sqrt{4.1})}{(3.5)^2 \times (3\frac{1}{2})^{-2}}$
i) $\dfrac{1\frac{1}{2} + \frac{1}{4}[(2\frac{2}{3})^2 - (1.4)^2]}{(3.9)^{-3}}$
j) $\sqrt[3]{2.73} + 5\sqrt{2}$

UNIT THREE

Standard Index Form

Writing very big (or very small) numbers gets a bit messy with all those zeros if you don't use this standard index form. But of course, the main reason for knowing about standard form is... you guessed it — it's in the Exam.

Q1 Write as ordinary numbers:

a) 3.56×10 e) 0.082×10^2 i) 157×10

b) 3.56×10^3 f) 0.082×10^{-2} j) 157×10^{-3}

c) 3.56×10^{-1} g) 0.082×10 k) 157×10^3

d) 3.56×10^4 h) 0.082×10^{-1} l) 157×10^{-1}.

Q2 Write in standard form:

a) 2.56   e) 95.2   i) 4200

b) 25.6   f) 0.0952   j) 0.0042

c) 0.256   g) 95 200   k) 42

d) 25 600   h) 0.000952   l) 420.

Q3 Write in standard form:

a) 34.7×10 e) 15 million   i) 534×10^{-2}

b) 73.004   f) 937.1×10^4 j) 621.03

c) 0.005×10^3 g) 0.000075   k) 149×10^2

d) 9183×10^2 h) 0.05×10^{-2} l) 0.003×10^{-4} .

Write the numbers in Questions 4 to 7 in standard form.

Q4 The distance between Paris and Rome is 1476 km.

Q5 A billion = a thousand million   A trillion = a thousand billion.

Q6 A light year is 9,460,000,000,000 km (approx).

Q7 Nautilus covered 69,138 miles before having to refuel.

Q8 A rectangular field is 24,700 cm by 15,000 cm.
What is its perimeter in m? Give your answer in standard form.

Q9 This table gives the diameter and distance from the Sun of some planets.

Planet	Distance from Sun (km)	Diameter (km)
Earth	1.5×10^8	1.3×10^4
Venus	1.085×10^8	1.2×10^4
Mars	2.28×10^8	6.8×10^3
Mercury	5.81×10^7	4.9×10^3
Jupiter	7.8×10^8	1.4×10^5
Neptune	4.52×10^9	4.9×10^4
Saturn	1.43×10^9	1.2×10^5

From the table write down which planet is:

a) smallest in diameter

b) largest in diameter

c) nearest to the Sun

d) furthest from the Sun.

Write down which planets are:

e) nearer to the Sun than the Earth

f) bigger in diameter than the Earth.

UNIT THREE

Basic Algebra

Q1 Work out the following temperature changes:
 a) 20 °C to -7 °C
 b) -10 °C to -32 °C
 c) -17 °C to -5 °C
 d) -3 °C to 15 °C
 e) -31 °C to -16 °C
 f) -5 °C to -17 °C

Q2 Which is larger and by how much?
 a) -12 + 7 – 4 + 6 – 2 + 7 or b) -30 + 26 – 3 – 7 + 17

Q3 Simplify: a) $4x - 5x + 3x - x + 2x - 7x$ b) $30y - 10y + 2y - 3y + 4y - 5y$

Q4 Find the value of xy and $\dfrac{x}{y}$ for each of the following:
 a) $x = -100$ $y = 10$
 b) $x = 24$ $y = -4$
 c) $x = -48$ $y = -3$
 d) $x = 0$ $y = -4$

Q5 Find the value of $(a - b) \div (c + d)$ when $a = 10$, $b = -26$, $c = -5$ and $d = -4$.

Q6 Simplify the following:
 a) $2x \times -3y$
 b) $-8a \times 2b$
 c) $-4x \times -2x$
 d) $4p \times -4p$
 e) $-30x \div -3y$
 f) $50x \div -5y$
 g) $10x \div -2y$
 h) $-30x \div -10x$
 i) $40ab \div -10ab$
 j) $70x^2 \div -7x^2$
 k) $-36x^2 \div -9x$
 l) $40y^2 \div -5y$

Q7 Simplify the following by collecting like terms together:
 a) $3x^2 + 4x + 12x^2 - 5x$
 b) $14x^2 - 10x - x^2 + 5x$
 c) $12 - 4x^2 + 10x - 3x^2 + 2x$
 d) $20abc + 12ab + 10bac + 4b$
 e) $8pq + 7p + q + 10qp - q + p$
 f) $15ab - 10a + b - 7a + 2ba$
 g) $4pq - 14p - 8q + p - q + 8p$
 h) $13x^2 + 4x^2 - 5y^2 + y^2 - x^2$
 i) $11ab + 2cd - ba - 13dc + abc$
 j) $3x^2 + 4xy + 2y^2 - z^2 + 2xy - y^2 - 5x^2$

Q8 Multiply out the brackets and simplify where possible:
 a) $4(x + y - z)$
 b) $x(x + 5)$
 c) $-3(x - 2)$
 d) $7(a + b) + 2(a + b)$
 e) $3(a + 2b) - 2(2a + b)$
 f) $4(x - 2) - 2(x - 1)$
 g) $4e(e + 2f) + 2f(e - f)$
 h) $14(2m - n) + 2(3n - 6m)$
 i) $4x(x + 2) - 2x(3 - x)$
 j) $3(2 + ab) + 5(1 - ab)$
 k) $(x - 2y)z - 2x(x + z)$
 l) $4(x - 2y) - (5 + x - 2y)$
 m) $a - 4(a + b)$
 n) $4pq(2 + r) + 5qr(2p + 7)$
 o) $x^2(x + 1)$
 p) $4x^2\left(x + 2 + \dfrac{1}{x}\right)$
 q) $8ab(a + 3 + b)$
 r) $7pq\left(p + q - \dfrac{1}{p}\right)$
 s) $4[(x + y) - 3(y - x)]$

Q9 For each of the large rectangles below, write down the area of each of the small rectangles and hence find an expression for the area of each large rectangle.
 a)
 b)
 c)

Eeeek — loads of questions...

Q10 All the expressions below have a^2 as a common factor. Factorise each of them.
 a) $a^2b + a^2c$
 b) $5a^2 + 13a^2b$
 c) $2a^2b + 3a^2c$
 d) $a^3 + a^2y$
 e) $2a^2x + 3a^2y + 4a^2z$
 f) $a^2b^2 + a^3c^2$

Algebraic Fractions & D.O.T.S.

Q1 Using the fact that $a^2 - b^2 = (a + b)(a - b)$, factorise the following expressions:

a) $x^2 - 9$

b) $y^2 - 16$

c) $25 - z^2$

d) $36 - a^2$

e) $4x^2 - 9$

f) $9y^2 - 4$

g) $25 - 16z^2$

h) $1 - 36a^2$

i) $x^4 - 36$

j) $x^4 - y^4$

k) $1 - (ab)^2$

l) $100\,x^2 - 144y^2$

Q2 Factorise:

a) $x^2 - 4$

b) $144 - y^4$

c) $1 - 9x^2y^2$

d) $49x^4y^4 - 1$

Q3 Simplify the following by cancelling down where possible:

a) $\dfrac{27x^4y^2z}{9x^3yz^2}$

b) $\dfrac{48a^2b^2}{(2a)^2 c}$

c) $\dfrac{3xyz}{9x^2y^3z^4}$

d) $\dfrac{4p^3q^3}{(2pr)^3}$

Q4 Multiply out the following, leaving your answers as simplified as possible:

a) $\dfrac{x^2}{y} \times \dfrac{2}{x^3}$

b) $\dfrac{3a^4}{2} \times \dfrac{b}{a^2}$

c) $\dfrac{2x}{y^2} \times \dfrac{y^3}{4x^3}$

d) $\dfrac{3pq}{2} \times \dfrac{4r^2}{9p}$

e) $\dfrac{10z^3}{xy} \times \dfrac{4x^3}{5z}$

f) $\dfrac{30a^2b^2c^2}{7} \times \dfrac{21c^2}{ab^3}$

g) $\dfrac{4}{x} \times \dfrac{x^3}{2} \times \dfrac{x}{10}$

h) $\dfrac{2a^2}{3} \times \dfrac{9b}{a} \times \dfrac{2a^2b}{5}$

i) $\dfrac{5a^2b}{b} \times \dfrac{3a^2c^3}{10bd}$

j) $\dfrac{p^2}{pq^2} \times \dfrac{q^2}{p}$

k) $\dfrac{90r^2}{14t} \times \dfrac{7t^3}{30r}$

l) $\dfrac{400d^4}{51e^5} \times \dfrac{102d^2e^4}{800e^2 f}$

It helps if you can cancel some factors before multiplying.

Q5 Divide the following, leaving your answer as simplified as possible:

a) $\dfrac{4x^3}{y} \div \dfrac{2x}{y^2}$

b) $\dfrac{ab}{c} \div \dfrac{b}{c}$

c) $\dfrac{30x^3}{y^2} \div \dfrac{10x}{y}$

d) $\dfrac{pq}{r} \div \dfrac{2}{r}$

e) $\dfrac{e^2f^2}{5} \div \dfrac{ef}{10}$

f) $\dfrac{5x^3}{y} \div \dfrac{1}{y}$

g) $\dfrac{16xyz}{3} \div \dfrac{4x^2}{9}$

h) $\dfrac{20a^3}{b^3} \div \dfrac{5}{b^2}$

i) $\dfrac{25a^3}{b^3} \div \dfrac{5}{b^2}$

j) $\dfrac{4x}{y^4z^4} \div \dfrac{2}{y^2z^3}$

k) $\dfrac{3m}{2n^2} \div \dfrac{m}{4n}$

l) $\dfrac{70f^3}{g} \div \dfrac{10f^4}{g^2}$

Q6 Solve the following equations for x:

a) $\dfrac{20x^4y^2z^3}{7xy^5} \times \dfrac{14y^3}{40x^2z^3} = 5$

b) $\dfrac{48x^5y^2}{12z^3} \div \dfrac{16x^2y^2}{z^3} = 2$

UNIT THREE

Algebraic Fractions

OK, I guess it gets a bit tricky here — you've got to cross-multiply to get a common denominator before you can get anywhere with adding or subtracting.

Q1 Add the following, simplifying your answers:

a) $\dfrac{3}{2x} + \dfrac{y}{2x}$ e) $\dfrac{5x+2}{x} + \dfrac{2x+4}{x}$ i) $\dfrac{2x}{3} + \dfrac{2x}{4}$

b) $\dfrac{1}{x} + \dfrac{y}{x}$ f) $\dfrac{6x}{3} + \dfrac{2x+y}{6}$ j) $\dfrac{x}{6} + \dfrac{5x}{7}$

c) $\dfrac{4xy}{3z} + \dfrac{2xy}{3z}$ g) $\dfrac{x}{8} + \dfrac{2+y}{24}$ k) $\dfrac{x}{3} + \dfrac{x}{y}$

d) $\dfrac{(4x+2)}{3} + \dfrac{(2x-1)}{3}$ h) $\dfrac{x}{10} + \dfrac{y-1}{5}$ l) $\dfrac{zx}{4} + \dfrac{x+z}{y}$

Q2 Subtract the following, leaving your answers as simplified as possible:

a) $\dfrac{4x}{3} - \dfrac{5y}{3}$ e) $\dfrac{10+x^2}{4x} - \dfrac{x^2+11}{4x}$ i) $\dfrac{2b}{a} - \dfrac{b}{7}$

b) $\dfrac{4x+3}{y} - \dfrac{4}{y}$ f) $\dfrac{2x}{3} - \dfrac{y}{6}$ j) $\dfrac{(p+q)}{2} - \dfrac{3p}{5}$

c) $\dfrac{(8x+3y)}{2x} - \dfrac{(4x+2)}{2x}$ g) $\dfrac{z}{5} - \dfrac{2z}{15}$ k) $\dfrac{p-2q}{4} - \dfrac{2p+q}{2}$

d) $\dfrac{(9-5x)}{3x} - \dfrac{(3+x)}{3x}$ h) $\dfrac{4m}{n} - \dfrac{m}{3}$ l) $\dfrac{3x}{y} - \dfrac{4-x}{3}$

Q3 Simplify the following:

a) $\left(\dfrac{a}{b} \div \dfrac{c}{d}\right) \times \dfrac{ac}{bd}$ d) $\dfrac{m^2 n}{p} + \dfrac{mn}{p^2}$ g) $\dfrac{a+b}{a-b} + \dfrac{a-b}{a+b}$

b) $\dfrac{x^2+xy}{x} \times \dfrac{z}{xz+yz}$ e) $\dfrac{1}{x+y} + \dfrac{1}{x-y}$ h) $\dfrac{1}{4pq} \div \dfrac{1}{3pq}$

c) $\dfrac{(p+q)}{r} \times \dfrac{3}{2(p+q)}$ f) $\dfrac{2}{x} - \dfrac{3}{2x} + \dfrac{4}{3x}$ i) $\dfrac{x}{8} - \dfrac{x+y}{4} + \dfrac{x-y}{2}$

UNIT THREE

Perimeters and Areas

Q1 Calculate the area and perimeter of the rectangle.

Q2 Calculate the area and perimeter of the square.

Q3 In front of a <u>toilet</u> is a special mat that fits snugly around the base.

Using the diagram opposite:
a) Find the <u>length of braid</u> needed to be stitched all round its edge.
b) Find the <u>area</u> of fluffy wool carpet it will cover when placed in front of the toilet.

You need the two circle formulas here
— $C = \pi \times D$ and $A = \pi \times r^2$.

Q4 A rectangular dining room, with a width equal to half its length, needs carpet tiling.
a) Calculate the area of the floor, if its width is 12 m.
b) If carpet tiles are 50 cm by 50 cm squares, calculate how many tiles will be required.
c) If carpet tiles cost £4.99 per m², calculate the <u>cost</u> of tiling the dining room.

Q5 An attachment on a child's toy is made from plastic in the shape of an octagon with a square cut out.
By counting squares or otherwise, find the area of plastic needed to make 4 of these attachments.

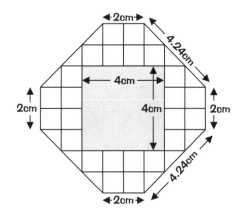

Q6 A cube bean bag is to be made out of material. If each side of the cube is to have edges of length 60 cm, how many <u>square metres</u> of material will be needed?

Q7 The area of a square is 9000 m².
a) What is the length of a <u>side</u>? (to 2 dp)
b) What is the <u>perimeter</u> of the square? (to 2 dp)

Q8 A fighter aircraft's wing is shown on the right. Calculate its <u>area</u>, and its <u>perimeter</u>.

Q9 A hanging basket bracket of sheet metal is stamped out in a 2 phase process:-
1st: The <u>outer triangle</u>, measuring 14.4 cm by 10 cm, is stamped out.
2nd: A smaller <u>inner triangle</u> measuring 5.76 cm by 4 cm is stamped out of the larger triangle.
How much metal makes up the finished bracket?

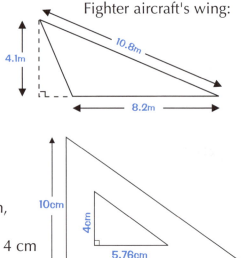

Unit Three

Volumes

Q1 Busy Buses Ltd decide to put a bus shelter near their main town centre stop. It is a prism with the dimensions shown.
a) Find the area of the cross-section of the shelter.
b) Find its volume.

Q2 Jill buys a bookshelf with the dimensions shown in the diagram.
a) Find the cross-sectional area.
b) Find the volume of the bookshelf in m³.

Q3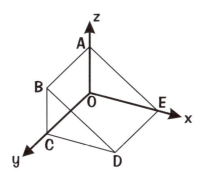

The diagram shows a triangular prism.
The coordinates of A are (0, 0, 5).
The coordinates of E are (4, 0, 0).
The coordinates of C are (0, 8, 0).
a) Write down the coordinates of:
  i) B
  ii) D.
b) Calculate the volume of the prism.

Q4 Bill bought a new garden shed with dimensions as shown. Find:
a) the area of the cross-section
b) the volume of the shed
c) the length AB
d) the total area of the roof.

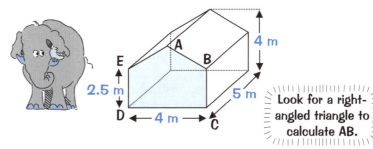

Look for a right-angled triangle to calculate AB.

Q5 A cuboid has a height of x m, a width of $(3 - x)$ m and a length of $(5 - x)$ m.
a) Write down an expression for the volume of the cuboid.
b) Complete the table of values using your expression for the volume of the cuboid.
c) Draw a graph of V against x for $0 \leqslant x \leqslant 3$.
d) Use your graph to estimate the maximum volume of the cuboid.
e) Estimate the surface area of the cuboid when the volume is at its maximum.
f) A particular cuboid has a volume of 6 m³. By using your graph to find the two possible values of x, estimate the maximum total surface area of the cuboid for this volume.

x	0	1	2	3
V			6	

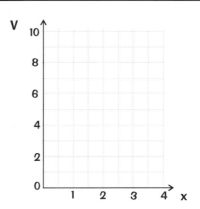

UNIT THREE

Solids and Nets

Before you go any further — make sure you know these 3 facts...

Surface Area and Nets

1) SURFACE AREA only applies to solid 3-D objects. It's the TOTAL AREA of all the OUTER SURFACES added together.
2) A NET is just A SOLID SHAPE folded out FLAT.
3) SURFACE AREA OF SOLID = AREA OF NET.

There are 4 nets that you need to know inside out... so to speak:
1) Triangular Prism, 2) Cube, 3) Cuboid, 4) Pyramid. I reckon you shouldn't read any further till you're 100% happy with them.

Q1 The net shown will fold to make a cube. Only one flap is shown. Copy the diagram.

a) Put an X in each corner that touches Y when the cube is made up.
b) Put an F where the flap will join one face to another, when the cube is made up.
c) Put on the other flaps necessary to glue the cube together.

Q2 Draw an accurate 2-dimensional net that would fold to make the 3-D cuboid shown (diagram is not full size). It is not necessary to include flaps.

Q3 Draw a full size net (without flaps) of a square-based pyramid whose base has sides of length 3 cm.

Q4 Draw accurately the net of a regular tetrahedron, with sufficient flaps to glue it together.

Q5 a) What shape is the base of the cuboid shown opposite?
b) Which edges are the same length as DE?
c) Which lengths equal CE?
d) Which lengths equal the diagonal DG?
e) How many vertices does the cuboid have?

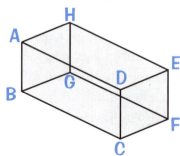

Q6 Draw a circular cone.
a) How many vertices does it have?
b) How many edges?

Q7 An equilateral triangular prism has a tetrahedron placed on top of it, as shown. For this combined solid,
a) How many edges does it have?
b) How many vertices?
c) How many faces?

UNIT THREE

Geometry

Here are some angle rules then — just the 7 for now. You can't get away without knowing these, I'm afraid, so get learning.

1) Angles in a triangle add up to 180°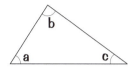

2) Angles in a 4-sided shape add up to 360°

3) Angles round a point add up to 360°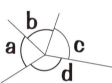

4) When a line crosses TWO PARALLEL LINES, the two bunches of angles are the same

5) Angles on a straight line add up to 180°

6) ISOSCELES TRIANGLES have two sides the same and two angles the same

7) EXTERIOR angle of a triangle = sum of opposite INTERIOR angles.

$d = a + b$

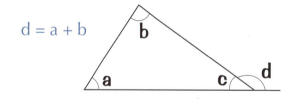

For the following diagrams, find the lettered angles. LM is a straight line.

Q1 a) b) c) d)

Q2 a) b) c) d)

UNIT THREE

Geometry

 This page is a bit dull — just lots of boring angles... still, that's geometry for you. Oh and by the way, you've got to work the angles out — don't try and sneakily measure them, they're probably drawn wrong anyway...

For the following diagrams, find the <u>lettered</u> angles.   LM is a straight line.

Q3 a) b) c) d)

Q4 a) b) c)

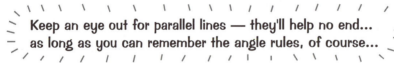
Keep an eye out for parallel lines — they'll help no end... as long as you can remember the angle rules, of course...

Q5 a) b) c)

Q6 a) b) c)

  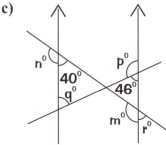

UNIT THREE

2D and 3D Coordinates

Q1 ABCD is a <u>parallelogram</u>. A is (-1, 3), B is (-2,-1) and C is (4,-1).
Draw axes with *x* from -3 to 5 and *y* from -2 to 4.
Plot A, B and C then find the <u>missing coordinates</u> for D.

Q2 Draw axes with *x* from -9 to 9 and *y* from -12 to 12.
On the <u>same</u> set of axes draw the following shapes and find their <u>missing pair of coordinates</u>.

a) ABCD is a <u>square</u>
A is (1, 1)
B is ?
C is (-3,-3)
D is (-3, 1)

b) ABCD is a <u>parallelogram</u>
A is (2, 8)
B is (6, 8)
C is ?
D is (1, 5)

c) ABCD is a <u>rectangle</u>
A is ?
B is (3,-8)
C is (3,-6)
D is (-5,-6)

d) ABCD is a <u>kite</u>
A is (-9, 3)
B is (-6, 8)
C is (-4, 8)
D is ?

e) ABCD is a <u>parallelogram</u>
A is (-2,-10)
B is (4,-10)
C is (6,-12)
D is ?

f) ABCD is a <u>parallelogram</u>
A is (-8, 10)
B is (-6, 10)
C is ?
D is (-5, 12)

Q3 ABCD is a <u>rectangle</u> with the line $x = 0$ as a <u>line of symmetry</u>.
Draw axes with *x* from -3 to 3 and *y* from -3 to 3.
If A = (-2,-2) and B is (-2, 1), find the <u>coordinates of C and D</u>.

I'm afraid you'll just have to get the hang of using things like "the line $x = 4$", as they seem to prefer it to "a vertical line through the point 4 on the horizontal axis". Yeah, that is a bit long winded, I guess — so maybe they've got a point...

Q4 Find the midpoint of the line AB, where A and B have coordinates:

a) A(2,3) B(4,5)
b) A(1,8) B(10,2)
c) A(0,11) B(11,11)
d) A(3,15) B(14,3)
e) A(6,7) B(0,0)
f) A(16,16) B(3,3)
g) A(8,33) B(32,50)
h) A(17,28) B(44,13)

Q5 The diagram shows a cuboid. Vertices A and H have coordinates (1, 2, 8) and (4, 5, 3) respectively.
Write down the coordinates of all the other vertices.

B (.... , ... , ...)
C (.... , ... , ...)
D (.... , ... , ...)
E (.... , ... , ...)
F (.... , ... , ...)
G (.... , ... , ...)

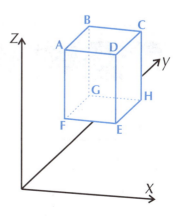

UNIT THREE

Straight Line Graphs

Q1 Which letters represent the following lines:

a) $x = y$
b) $x = 5$
c) $y = -x$
d) $x = 0$
e) $y = -7$
f) $x + y = 0$
g) $y = 5$
h) $x - y = 0$
i) $y = 0$
j) $x = -7$?

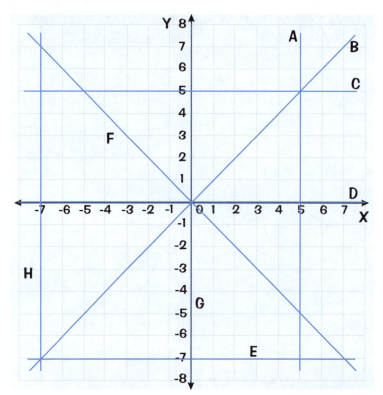

Don't get confused if you've got "x + y = ..." — just rearrange the equation to "y = -x + ..." and as if by magic, you've got a line you recognise.

Q2 Complete the following table for the line $y = 3x - 1$:

x	-4	-3	-2	-1	0	1	2	3	4
3x									
-1									
y									

Plot these points on graph paper and hence draw the graph of $y = 3x - 1$.
Use a scale of 1 cm for 2 units on the y axis and 2 cm for 1 unit on the x axis.

Q3 Complete the following table for the line $y = \frac{1}{2}x - 3$:

x	-6	-4	-2	0	2	4	6
½ x							
-3							
y							

Plot these points on graph paper and hence draw the graph of $y = \frac{1}{2}x - 3$.

Straight Line Graphs

If you know it's a straight line, you only really need <u>two</u> points, but it's always a <u>good idea</u> to plot three — it's a bit of a safety net, really.

Q4 Complete this table of values for $y = 2x + 3$:

x	0	3	8
y			

Plot these points on graph paper and draw the graph of $y = 2x + 3$.
Use your graph to find:

a) The value of y when $x = 5$
b) The value of y when $x = 2$
c) The value of x when $y = 11$
d) The value of x when $y = 17$

Q5 Complete this table of values for $y = \frac{1}{4}x - 3$:

x	-8	-4	8
y			

Plot these points on graph paper and draw the graph of $y = \frac{1}{4}x - 3$.
Use your graph to find:

a) The value of y when $x = 2$
b) The value of y when $x = 0$
c) The value of x when $y = -2$
d) The value of x when $y = -1.5$

Q6 The cost of electricity is calculated using the formula:
Total cost = Fixed charge + (cost per unit × number of units).

Customers can choose two different methods of payment:
Method A: Fixed charge £10, cost per unit 25p
Method B: Fixed charge £40, cost per unit 5p
Copy and complete this table:

Number of Units used	0	100	200	300
Cost using method A				
Cost using method B				

Plot these points on a graph (put the number of units on the horizontal axis, cost on the vertical axis):

a) Use your graph to find the total cost when 70 units are used for:
   i) Method A
   ii) Method B
b) Miss Wright used 75 units. Which method should she use to minimize her bill, Method A or Method B?
c) Mr Jones and Mrs Green both used exactly the same number of units and paid the same amount. Mr Jones used Method A, Mrs Green used Method B. How many units did they each use?

UNIT THREE

UNIT FOUR

46

Surds Mostly

Q1 Write down the reciprocals of the following values.
Leave your answers as whole numbers or fractions.

a) 7 **b)** 12 **c)** $\dfrac{3}{8}$ **d)** $-\dfrac{1}{2}$

Q2 Use your calculator to work out the reciprocals of the following values.
Write your answers as whole numbers or decimals.

a) 12 **b)** $\sqrt{2}$ **c)** π **d)** 0.008

Q3 If Monsieur Abbé employs twice as many grape-pickers to harvest his vineyard, the job will be done twice as fast. Are the number of grape-pickers and the time it takes for the vineyard to be harvested **directly** or **indirectly** proportional?

Q4 A circle has a radius of $\sqrt{3}$ cm. What is its exact area? (Area of circle = πr^2)

Q5 Simplify:

Remember — $\sqrt{a} \times \sqrt{b} = \sqrt{(ab)}$.

a) $\sqrt{5} \times \sqrt{3}$ **b)** $\dfrac{\sqrt{20}}{\sqrt{5}}$ **c)** $\sqrt{4} - \sqrt{1}$ **d)** $\left(\dfrac{\sqrt{5}}{\sqrt{2}}\right)^2$

e) $\left(\sqrt{x}\right)^2$ **f)** $\sqrt{x^2}$ **g)** $\sqrt{8} \times \sqrt{8}$ **h)** $\sqrt{18} - \sqrt{9}$

Q6 If $x = 1$ and $y = \sqrt{2}$, are the following expressions rational or irrational?

a) $(x + y)(x - y)$ **b)** $\dfrac{x + y}{x - y}$

Q7 Rationalise the denominators of the following expressions, and then simplify if necessary.

a) $\dfrac{1}{\sqrt{2}}$ **b)** $\dfrac{2}{\sqrt{8}}$ **c)** $\dfrac{a}{\frac{\sqrt{40}}{2}}$ **d)** $\dfrac{x}{\sqrt{xy}}$

e) $\dfrac{1}{1 + \sqrt{2}}$ **f)** $\dfrac{6}{3 + \sqrt{3}}$ **g)** $\dfrac{2}{1 + \sqrt{6}}$ **h)** $\dfrac{5 + \sqrt{5}}{5 - \sqrt{5}}$

Remember: rationalising the denominator means getting rid of the square root signs on the bottom of fractions.

UNIT FOUR

Ratios

I don't want to spoil the surprise, but you're going to need your calculator for this bit — get your finger on that fraction button...

RATIOS are like FRACTIONS which are like DECIMALS

We can treat the RATIO 3:4 like the FRACTION ¾, which is 0.75 as a DECIMAL.

Watch out though — this isn't ¾ of the total:

If there are girls and boys in the ratio 3:4, it means there's ¾ as many girls as boys.

So if there's 8 boys, there's ¾ × 8 = 6 girls.

Q1 Write these ratios in their simplest forms:
- a) 6:8
- b) 5:20
- c) 1.5:3
- d) 2¼: 4
- e) 2 weeks: 4 days
- f) £1.26:14p

Q2 A rectangle has sides in the ratio 1:2. Calculate the length of the longer side if the shorter side is:
- a) 3 cm
- b) 5.5 cm
- c) 15.2 m

Calculate the length of the shorter side if the longer side is:
- d) 3 cm
- e) 5.5 cm
- f) 15.2 m

Q3 Divide the following amounts in the ratios given:
- a) £20 in the ratio 2:3
- b) 150 m in the ratio 8:7
- c) 500 g in the ratio 1:2:2
- d) 8 hrs in the ratio 1:2:3

For these you add up the ratio numbers to find the total number of parts and divide by this. Then multiply by each number in the ratio separately to find the different amounts.

Q4
- a) Increase £3.20 in the ratio 2:3.
- b) Decrease 120 cm in the ratio 3:2.

Q5 John and Peter share a bar of chocolate marked into 16 squares. They share it in the ratio 1:3. How many squares does each boy get?

Q6 A 2 litre bottle of cola is to be shared between three girls in the ratio 2:3:5. How many millilitres will each girl get?

Watch out for your units — you'll have to change them over for this one — and your answer should be in millilitres.

Q7 Oak and ash saplings are planted along a roadside in the ratio 2:3 respectively. If there are 20 oak saplings, how many ash saplings are there?

Q8 Tony gives £100 to be shared by Jane, Paul and Rosemary in a ratio according to their age. Jane is 10, Paul is 12 and Rosemary is 3 years old. How much will each child get?

UNIT FOUR

Calculations — Upper Bounds and Powers

Q1 $R = \dfrac{S}{T}$ is a formula used by stockbrokers.

S=940, correct to 2 significant figures and T=5.56, correct to 3 significant figures.

a) For the value of S, write down the upper bound and the lower bound.
b) For the value of T, write down the upper bound and the lower bound.
c) Calculate the upper bound and lower bound for R.
d) Write down the value of R correct to an appropriate number of significant figures.

Q2 A lorry travelled 125 kilometres in 1 hour and 50 minutes. If the time was measured to the nearest 10 minutes and the distance to the nearest five kilometres, what was the maximum value of the average speed of the lorry, in kilometres per hour?

Remember — you don't always get the maximum value by using the biggest input value.

Q3 Find the value of the following, giving your answers in <u>standard form</u>.
a) $46 \times 4.2 \times 5000$ **c)** $0.2 \times 0.3 \times 0.5 \times 0.1$ **e)** $62000 \div 0.31$
b) $20 \times 4 \times 5 \times 8.2$ **d)** $5000 \div 0.02$ **f)** $40000000 \div 1000$

Q4 Given that $p = 2.3$, $q = 3\frac{1}{2}$, $r = -1.2$, calculate:
a) $p^2 + q^3$
b) $p^{-2} + q^{\frac{1}{2}} + r^2$
c) $(p + q)^2 - r^{\frac{1}{3}}$
d) $p^{\frac{2}{3}} - q^{\frac{1}{3}}$
e) $(q - r)^3 - p^4$
f) $q^{\frac{2}{3}} + r^{\frac{1}{4}}$
g) $q^{-2} + r^3$
h) $p^{-2} + q^{\frac{1}{2}} - r^3$.

No calculators for the rest of these questions...

Q5 Find the <u>value of n</u> where $12^5 \div 12^n = 12^7$

Q6 Find the <u>reciprocal</u> of 1000 and express as a power of 10.

Q7 Which of the following are <u>true</u>?
a) $2^{-3} = 1/6$ **c)** $4^{-2} = 1/16$ **e)** $1/9 = 3^2$
b) $17^0 = 0$ **d)** $1^{-17} = 1$ **f)** $28^0 = 1$

Q8 Write as a <u>single power</u>:
a) $2^4 \times 2^{-3}$ **c)** $8^3 \div 8^1$ **e)** $x^4 \div x^{-1}$ **g)** $3^{-2} \times (3^{-4} \div 3^0)$
b) $2^6 \times 2^0$ **d)** $4^6 \div 4^{-2}$ **f)** $y^3 \div y^2$ **h)** $(3^{-2})^3$

Q9 Find the numbers replaced by x in these statements:
a) $3^x = 9$ **c)** $10^x = 1000$ **e)** $17^x = 1$ **g)** $(4^2)^x = 4^6$ **i)** $8^x = 1/8$
b) $3^x = 1/9$ **d)** $4^x = 1/16$ **f)** $3^x \times 3^{-1} = 3^5$ **h)** $(5^x)^2 = 5^6$ **j)** $x^5 = 1$

UNIT FOUR

Fractions

Q1 Without using a calculator, write the following fractions as decimals:

a) $\dfrac{14}{8}$ b) $\dfrac{8}{64}$ c) $\dfrac{24}{40}$ d) $\dfrac{4}{80}$

Q2 Write the following fractions as recurring decimals:

a) $\dfrac{10}{11}$ b) $\dfrac{29}{33}$ c) $\dfrac{478}{999}$ d) $\dfrac{5891}{9999}$

Q3 Do these without a calculator, giving your answers in their lowest terms:

a) $1\tfrac{1}{4} \times 3\tfrac{1}{8}$ b) $1\tfrac{1}{4} \times 4\tfrac{1}{8}$ c) $1\tfrac{1}{4} \div 3\tfrac{1}{8}$

d) $1\tfrac{1}{4} + 3\tfrac{1}{8}$ e) $1\tfrac{1}{4} + 4\tfrac{1}{8}$ f) $3\tfrac{1}{8} - 1\tfrac{1}{4}$

Q4 Dwight scored 50 goals last season. 30 of these were scored at his home ground.
a) Write down the fraction (in its lowest terms) of goals scored at his home ground.
b) Calculate the fraction of goals scored away from home.

Q5 The population of Australia is 18 million, of which 3.5 million people live in Sydney and 1 million people live in Perth.
a) What fraction of the population live in Perth?
b) What fraction of the population live in Perth or Sydney?

Q6 A ball is dropped from a height of 6 m.

After each bounce the ball rises to $\dfrac{2}{3}$ of its previous height. What height will it reach after the third bounce?

Q7 George wants to make a cake. The recipe requires 150 g each of flour, sugar and butter, and 3 eggs. George only has 2 eggs so he decides to make a smaller cake with the same proportions of ingredients.

a) How much flour will George need to use?
b) If each egg weighs 25 g, how much will the cake weigh before it goes in the oven?
c) What fraction of the uncooked weight is flour?
d) If the cake loses one seventh of its weight during baking (due to moisture loss) what will it weigh after baking?

Unit Four

Percentages

Make sure you can switch from fractions to decimals to percentages before you start.

Q1 Express each percentage as a decimal:
 a) 50% b) 12% c) 40% d) 34%

Q2 Express each percentage as a fraction in its lowest terms:
 a) 25% b) 60% c) 45% d) 30%

Q3 Express each of the following as a percentage:
 a) $\frac{1}{8}$ b) 0.23 c) $\frac{12}{40}$ d) 0.34

Q4 In a French test, Lauren scored 17/20. What percentage is this?

Q5 87 out of 120 pupils at Backwater School have access to a computer. What percentage is this?

There are three types of percentage question. The first one is working out "something % of something else" — it's dead easy. Just remember to add it back on to the original amount if you've got a VAT question.

Q6 John bought a new video recorder. The tag in the shop said it cost £299 + VAT. If VAT is charged at 17½%, how much did he pay (to the nearest penny)?

Q7 Four friends stay at the Pickled Parrot Hotel for a night and each have an evening meal. Bed and Breakfast costs £37 per person and the evening meal costs £15 per person. How much is the total cost, if VAT is added at 17½%?

Q8 Donald earns an annual wage of £23 500. He doesn't pay tax on the first £3400 that he earns. How much income tax does he pay a year if the rate of tax is:
 a) 25%
 b) 40%?

Q9 Tanya paid £6500 for her new car. Each year its value decreased by 8%.
 a) How much was it worth when it was one year old?
 b) How much was it worth when it was two years old?

Q10 Jeremy wanted a new sofa for his lounge. A local furniture shop had just what he was looking for — and for only £130.00 + VAT. Jeremy had £150 pounds in his bank account. If VAT was charged at 17½%, could Jeremy afford the sofa?

Here's the 2nd type — finding "something as a percentage of something else" — in this case you're looking at percentage change, so don't forget to find the difference in values first.

Q11 During a rainstorm, a water butt increased in weight from 10.4 kg to 13.6 kg. What was the percentage increase (to the nearest per cent)?

UNIT FOUR

Percentages

Q12 An electrical store reduces the price of a particular camera from £90.00 to £78.30. What is the percentage reduction?

Q13 There are approximately 6000 fish and chip shops in the UK. On average, a fish and chip shop gets about 160 visitors each day. Given that the population of the UK is roughly 60 million, approximately what percentage of the population visit a fish and chip shop each day?

Q14 At birth, Veronica was 0.3 m tall. By adulthood she had grown to 1.5 m tall. Calculate her height now as a percentage of her height at birth.

Q15 Desmond's GCSE maths exam is next week. As part of his revision he attempted 31 questions on his least favourite topic of percentages. He got 21 questions fully right on the first attempt. Two days later he tried all 31 questions again and this time got 29 correct.
  a) What percentage of questions did he get correct on his first attempt?
  b) What percentage of questions did he get correct on his second attempt?
  c) What is the percentage improvement in Desmond's results?

Q16 I wish to invest £1000 for a period of three years and have decided to place my money with the Highrise Building Society on 1 January. If I choose to use the Gold Account I will withdraw the interest at the end of each year. If I choose to use the Silver Account I will leave the interest to be added to the capital at the end of each year.

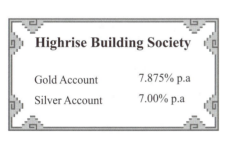

  a) Calculate the total interest I will receive if I use the Gold Account.
  b) Calculate the total interest I will receive if I use the Silver Account.
  After some thought I decide to use the Gold Account and leave the interest to be added to the capital at the end of each year.
  c) Calculate the total interest I will now receive from the Gold Account.

Q17 If L = MN, what is the percentage increase in L if M increases by 15% and N increases by 20%?

Ooh... here's the 3rd type — finding the <u>original value</u>. The bit most people get wrong is deciding whether the value given represents <u>more</u> or <u>less than 100%</u> of the original — so <u>always</u> check your answer <u>makes sense</u>.

Q18 In the new year sales Robin bought a tennis racket for £68.00. The original price had been reduced by 15%. What was the original price?

Q19 There are 360 people living in a certain village. The population of the village has grown by 20% over the past year.
  a) How many people lived in the village one year ago?
  b) If the village continues to grow at the same rate, how many whole years from today will it be before the population is more than twice its current size?

UNIT FOUR

D/T Graphs and V/T Graphs

You need to remember what the different bits of a travel graph mean — what it looks like when <u>stopped</u>, <u>changing speed</u> and <u>coming back</u> to the starting point.

Q1 This diagram shows the different times taken by 5 trains to travel 100 km.
  a) Calculate the speed of each train.
  b) How could you tell by looking at the diagram which was the fastest and which was the slowest?
  c) Train D should have been travelling at 50 km/h. How many minutes late was it?

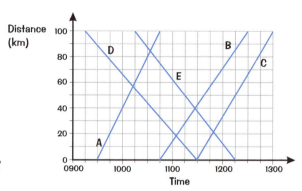

Q2 On sports day the first three in the 1000 m race ran as shown in the graph below.
  a) Which runner, A, B or C, won the race?
  b) How long did the winner take?
  c) Which runner kept up a steady speed?
  d) What was that speed
    i) in m/min?
    ii) km/h?
  e) Which runner achieved the fastest speed and what was that speed?

Q3 Two cars start a journey at midday (1200) — one travels from town A to village B, and the other from village B to town A. A and B are 80 km apart. The car from town A travels at an average speed of 48 km/h and the other car, from village B, at 60 km/h.
  a) Draw a graph to show these journeys.
  b) At what time do the cars pass? (approx.)
  c) How far from A are they when they pass?

Use the speeds given to work out the time it takes for each car to travel the 80 km.

Q4 A girl set off on an all-day walk. She started at 0915 and walked at a steady speed for 9 km before stopping at 1100 for a 20 min break. She then set off again at a steady speed and walked 8 km, stopping at 1300 for 45 mins. After lunch she walked at 3½ km/h for 2½ hrs to her destination.
  a) Draw a graph to show this walk.
  b) How far did she walk altogether?
  c) What was the average speed for the whole walk?
  d) What was her fastest walking speed?

UNIT FOUR

Regular Polygons

The one thing they're <u>guaranteed</u> to ask you about is <u>Interior and Exterior Angles</u> — you'd better get learning those formulas...

> A <u>**POLYGON**</u> is a many-sided shape. A <u>**REGULAR**</u> polygon is one where **ALL THE SIDES AND ANGLES ARE THE SAME**.
>
> You need to know these two formulas:
> 1) EXTERIOR ANGLE = 360° ÷ No. of Sides
> 2) INTERIOR ANGLE = 180° − EXTERIOR ANGLE

Q1 What sort of triangles occur in every <u>regular polygon</u> (<u>except</u> a hexagon), when each vertex is joined to the centre by a straight line?

Q2 Using a compass, construct an <u>equilateral</u> triangle with sides 3 cm. What is the interior angle at each vertex?

Q3 Sketch a regular hexagon and draw in all its lines of symmetry. State the order of <u>rotational</u> symmetry.

Q4 In each of the pentagons below, all the sides are of equal length, two of the angles are 90° and the other interior angles are m, m, and r degrees.

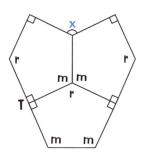

a) Explain in <u>two</u> different ways why 2m + r = 360°.
b) What is the size of exterior angle x?
c) Copy the diagram and add two more pentagons (by tracing through) so that the point T is completely surrounded and the whole figure forms part of a tessellation. Label all the angles of the new pentagons.

Q5 A square and a regular hexagon are placed adjacent to each other.

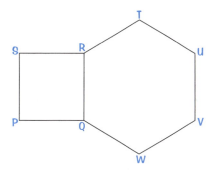

a) What is the <u>size</u> of ∠PQW?
b) What is the <u>size</u> of ∠PRW?
c) How many sides has the <u>regular polygon</u> that has ∠PQW as one of its angles?

Q6 An <u>irregular pentagon</u> has interior angles of 100°, 104°, 120°. If the other two angles are equal, what is their size?

Q7 a) The <u>sum</u> of the <u>interior</u> angles of a <u>regular</u> 24-sided polygon is 3960°. Use this to calculate the size of one <u>interior</u> angle.
b) From your answer to part **a)** calculate one <u>exterior</u> angle and show that the <u>sum</u> of the exterior angles equals 360°.

Unit Four

Regular Polygons

Q8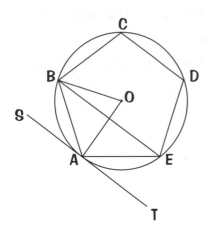
ABCDE is a regular pentagon. It is drawn in a circle centre O. SAT is a tangent drawn to the circle at A.
a) Calculate the size of angle BOA.
b) Find the size of angle OBA.
c) Write down the size of angle:
  i) SAO
  ii) BAS.
d) Hence write down the size of angle BEA giving a reason for your answer.

Q9 The sum of the interior angles of a regular polygon is 2520°. How many sides does this regular polygon have?

Remember that formula for the sum of interior angles — it comes in handy here.

Q10 a) Describe fully the transformation that would map triangle ABO onto triangle DEO so that A mapped onto D, B onto E and O remained unchanged.
b) Describe fully the transformation that would map triangle ABO onto triangle EDO so that A mapped onto E, B onto D and O remained unchanged.
c) Describe fully the transformation that would map triangle ABO onto triangle BOC so that A mapped onto B, B mapped onto C and O remained unchanged.

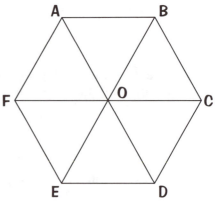
ABCDEF is a regular hexagon.

Q11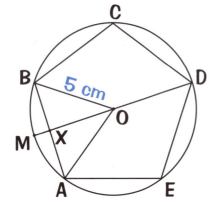
ABCDE is a regular pentagon whose vertices lie on a circle of radius 5 cm, centre O. DOM is an axis of symmetry of the pentagon and cuts the chord AB at X.
a) Calculate the size of angle BOX.
b) Find the length OX. Hence find the distance of M from the chord AB.

You need to use trigonometry to find OX — Cos θ = adj / hyp.

Q12 ABCDEFGH is a regular octagon.
a) Copy the figure and mark on the axis of symmetry which maps H to A.
b) Calculate the size of angle EFC.

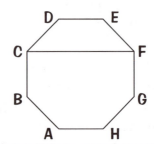

Circle Geometry

Q1 Using π = 3.14, find:
a) The area of a circle with radius = 6.12 m. Give your answer to 3 dp.
b) The circumference of a circle with radius = 7.2 m. Give your answer to 2 sf.
c) The circumference of a circle with diameter = 14.8 m. Give your answer to 1 dp.
d) The area of a circle with diameter = 4.246 cm. Give answer your to 3 dp.

Q2 Find the area and the perimeter of each of the shapes drawn here. Use π = 3.14.

a)   b)   c)

Q3 A plastic strip is made in the shape shown. The curves AC and BD are both arcs of circles with centre O. The larger circle has radius 30 mm and the smaller circle has radius 20 mm. The shaded ends of the shape are both semicircles.

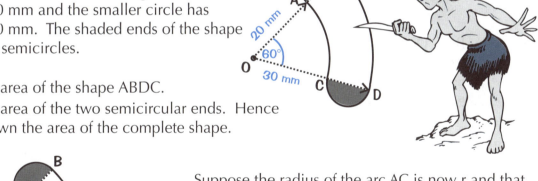

a) Find the area of the shape ABDC.
b) Find the area of the two semicircular ends. Hence write down the area of the complete shape.

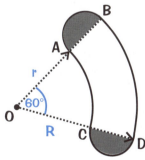

Suppose the radius of the arc AC is now r and that of BD is R.

c) Write down a formula for the area of the sector OBD in terms of R.
d) Write down an expression for the area of the shape ABDC in terms of r and R.
e) Hence write down an expression for the area of the complete shape.

Q4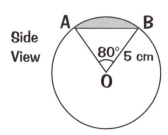

A washing powder ball looks from the side like a circle with the shaded area removed. The circle has radius 5 cm and the angle AOB = 80°.

a) Find the area of the sector OAB.
b) Find the area of triangle AOB and hence the area of the shaded area.

The formula you need for part b) is area = ½absin(c).

UNIT FOUR

Circle Geometry

Q5 ABCD is a cyclic quadrilateral with angle BCD = 100°.
EF is a tangent to the circle touching it at A.
Angle DAF = 30°.
Write down the size of angle:
a) BAD
b) EAB.

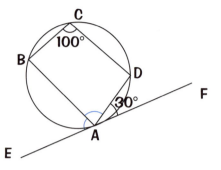

Q6 A, B, and C are points on the circumference of a circle with centre O. BD and CD are tangents of the circle.
a) State the length BD in the diagram on the right.
b) Calculate the angle COD.
c) State the angle COB.
d) Find the angle CAB.

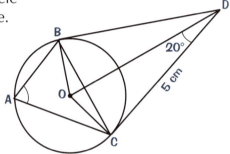

Q7 A, B, C, D and E are points on the circumference of a circle with centre O. Angle BDE = 53°. The line AF is a tangent to the circle, touching it at A. Angle EAF = 32°. Find:
a) angle BOE
b) angle ACE.

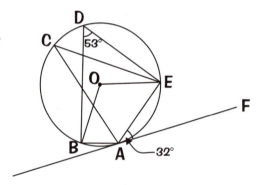

Q8 ABCD is a cyclic quadrilateral and the tangent to the circle at A makes an angle of 70° with the side AD. Angle BCA = 30°. Write down, giving a reason, the size of:
a) angle ACD
b) angle BAD.

Q9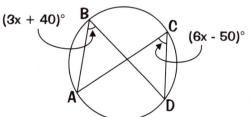

A, B, C and D are points on the circumference of a circle. Angle ABD = $(3x + 40)°$ and angle ACD = $(6x - 50)°$.
a) Give a reason why angle ABD and angle ACD are the same.
b) Form an equation in x and by solving it, find the size of angle ABD.

Circle Geometry

Q10 O is the centre of a circle and AB is a chord. The length OA = 5 cm and angle OAB = 20°. Find the length of the chord AB.

One way to do this is to work out angle AOB and use the sine rule.

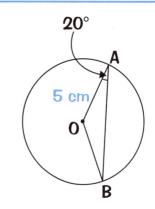

Q11 A, B, C and D are points on the circumference of a circle. O is the centre of the circle and angle AOD = 140°. Write down:
a) angle ABD
b) angle ABC
c) angle DBC.

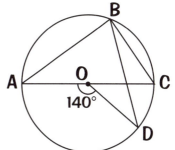

Q12 A tangent of a circle is drawn, touching it at A. C and B are two other points on the circumference and AOB is a diameter. O is the centre of the circle. Angle ABC is 23°.
a) Write down the size of angle ACB, giving a reason for your answer.
b) Find the size of the angle marked x° in the diagram.

Q13

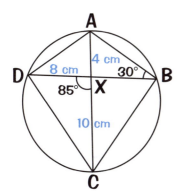

ABCD is a cyclic quadrilateral. The lines AC and BD intersect at X. Lengths AX = 4 cm, DX = 8 cm and XC = 10 cm. Angles DXC = 85° and ABD = 30°.
a) Show that triangles DXC and AXB are similar.
b) Find the length of XB.
c) Write down the size of angle BDC.

Q14 B, C and D are three points on the circumference of a circle with BD as a diameter. O is the centre of the circle and ADC is a straight line. AB = 10 cm and BC = 3 cm.
a) Write down the size of angle ACB, giving a reason for your answer.
b) Show that AC is 9.54 cm correct to 2 decimal places.
c) If AD = 5 cm, find the length of the diameter DOB correct to 2 decimal places.

UNIT FOUR

Surface Area and Volume

Make sure you know the 4 main volume formulas — for spheres, prisms, pyramids, cones.

Q1 a, b and h are lengths. Which of the following formulas could represent a volume? Give a reason for your answer.

  a) πabh
  b) $\pi(a + b)h$
  c) $\pi h^2(a + b)$
  d) $\pi h^2(a + b)^2$

Q2 Joe buys a garden cloche to protect his plants from frost. It has a semicircular diameter of 70 cm and a length of 3 m.
  a) Find the cross-sectional area.
  b) Hence find the volume of the cloche.

Q3 In my garden I have a circular pond which is surrounded by a ring shaped paved area. The pond is 35 cm deep and is filled with water.
  a) Find the volume of water in the pond when full.
  b) Find the area of paving surrounding the pond.

Q4 A solid metal cube, each of whose sides is 10 cm long, is melted down and made into a cylinder 10 cm high.
  a) What is the radius of this cylinder?
  b) Find the surface area of the cylinder.

Q5 A tin mug has the dimensions shown.
  a) What is the greatest volume of milk the mug can hold?
  b) In fact, 600 cm³ of milk is poured in. How high will it go up the mug?

Q6

A nut has the cross-section illustrated. The circular hole has a diameter of 1.4 cm and the nut is 5 mm thick.
Find the volume of the nut in cm³.

UNIT FOUR

Surface Area and Volume

Q7 Water is flowing into each of these containers at a constant rate.
For each container, sketch the graph of the depth of water against time.

Container A

Container B

Q8

An egg timer is symmetrical and consists of hemispheres, cylinders and cones joined together as shown to the left.

a) Calculate the volume of sand in the upper container.

You need to find three volumes and add them together.

Sand runs into the bottom container at a constant rate of 0.05 cm³ per second. At the end of a certain time period the sand has fallen through into the bottom container as shown to the right.

b) How high (h) has it risen up the cylindrical part of the bottom container?
c) How long has it taken the sand to fall through until it is at this height?

Q9

An ice-cream cone is 10 cm deep and has a base diameter of 5 cm. The bottom 4 cm of the cone is filled with solid chocolate as shown. The rest of the cone is filled with ice cream and a hemisphere of ice cream is mounted on top so that the base of the hemisphere coincides with the base of the cone.

a) Calculate the volume of ice cream required to make one ice cream.
b) Calculate the outer surface area of the cone.

Q10

A cylindrical container of diameter 10 cm and height 20 cm is filled with water to a depth of 10 cm. 3,200 identical ball bearings are now submerged in the water. The depth increases to 18 cm. Calculate the radius of one ball bearing.

The volume increase is a cylinder and you're told the height.

UNIT FOUR

Loci and Constructions

Don't let a silly word like <u>locus</u> put you off — there are <u>easy marks</u> to be had here, but you've got to do everything neatly, using a pencil, ruler and compasses.

Q1 Inside the rectangle:
a) draw the locus of points 5 cm from D
b) draw the locus of points equidistant from A and D
c) indicate by an X, the point inside the rectangle which is 5 cm from D and equidistant from A and D.

Q2 Construct triangle PQR accurately with length PQ = 10.5 cm, angle PQR = 95° and angle RPQ = 32°.
a) Draw in the perpendicular bisector of the line PR. Draw in point A where the bisector crosses the line PQ.
b) Bisect angle PRQ. Draw in point B where the bisector crosses the line PQ. Measure the length BA.

Q3 To win a bet, a man had to walk round his house remaining exactly 3 m from it all the way round.
Using a scale of 1 cm to 1 m draw the locus of the man's movement round the house, marking the walls of the house clearly on your diagram.

Q4 Construct triangle PQR with length PQ = QR = 11.5 cm and angle PQR = 38°.
a) Draw the bisectors of angles QPR and QRP. Mark the point O where the 2 bisectors cross.
b) With centre O draw the circle which just touches the sides PQ, PR and QR of the triangle. What is the radius of this circle?

Q5 A and B are 2 points on a straight shore, 4 km apart with A due west of B.
a) Describe the locus of points P such that angle APB equals 90°.
b) Using a scale of 2 cm to 1 km draw an accurate scale diagram showing A, B, the shore line and the locus of P.
An outcrop of rock is located on a bearing of 060° from A and 300° from B.
c) Indicate the rock on your diagram. Mark the spot with an X.
d) A ship steaming due east parallel to the shore avoids the rock by following the locus of P. How near does the ship come to the rock?

Think about your geometry rules.

UNIT FOUR

Loci and Constructions

Just to be really awkward, these points don't always make a nice line — they can cover a whole area... and you're gonna be asked to shade areas containing all the points.

Q6 This is a plan of Simon's room. To keep warm Simon must be within 2 m of the wall with the radiator on. To see out of the window he must be within 1.5 m of the wall containing the window.

a) Using a scale of 2 cm to 1 m draw a plan of Simon's room.

b) Shade the region in which Simon must be if he is to be warm and see out of the window.

Q7 A running track is designed so that each point on the track is 32.5 m from a fixed line AB which is 100 m long.

a) Draw the locus of the line.
b) Calculate the distance once round the running track.

Q8 The diagram shows a plan of Jim's back garden. Two sides of the garden are bounded by fences and the other sides are bounded by the walls of the house and garage. The garden is in the shape of a rectangle.

a) Using a scale of 1 cm to 1 m draw a plan of Jim's garden.

b) Ben, the friendly rottweiler, is tethered to the garage at B by a chain of length 3 m. Construct accurately and shade the part of the garden where Ben can go.

c) Jim wants to plant a tree in the garden. The tree must be planted more than 5 m away from the walls of the house and more than 4 m away from each fence. On the plan of the garden, construct accurately and shade the region where Jim can plant his tree.

Q9 The positions of two islands A and B are found from the following information: A is 35 km from a jetty J on a bearing 065°, B is due south of A and on a bearing of 132° from J as shown below.

a) Using a scale of 1 cm to 5 km, draw an accurate plan to show the positions of J, A and B.
b) Find from your drawing the distance in km between the islands A and B.
c) A boat leaves the jetty at 09.00 and reaches A at 11.30. What is its average speed in km/h?
d) A lightship L is 20 km from J, equidistant from A and B and on the same side of J as A and B. Mark L on the drawing.
e) Find the bearing of L from J.

UNIT FOUR

Congruence, Similarity and Enlargement

Q1 Which pair of triangles are congruent? Explain why.

Q2 In the diagram below, BC is parallel to DE.
AB = 12 cm, BD = 8 cm, DE = 25 cm and CE = 10 cm.

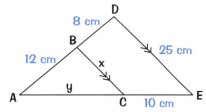

a) Explain why triangles ABC and ADE are similar.
b) Find the lengths of x and y in the diagram.

Q3 Another triangle, congruent to the triangle shown on the right, must be drawn with vertices at three of the dots. Show in how many different ways this can be done.

 Don't forget that when you're enlarging areas and volumes, there's a bigger scale factor — that one catches everyone out, believe me...

Q4 Two cups A and B are similar. Cup A has a height of 15 cm and cup B has a height of 10 cm. Cup A has a volume of 54 cm³. Calculate the volume of cup B.

Q5 A cylindrical bottle can hold 1 litre of oil. A second cylindrical bottle has twice the radius but the same height. It also contains oil.
 a) Explain why these bottles are not similar.
 b) How much oil can the larger bottle hold?

Q6 A boy made a symmetrical framework with metal rods as shown. Lengths AB = BC, ST = TC and AP = PQ. Angle BVC = 90° and length BV = 9 cm.
 a) Find two triangles which are similar to triangle ABC.
 b) Calculate the length of AP. Hence write down the length of PT.
 c) Calculate the area of triangle ABC.
 d) Find the area of triangle APQ. Give your answer correct to 3 significant figures.
 e) Hence write down the area of PQBST correct to 2 significant figures.

Unit Four

Symmetry

They do say that bad things happen in threes... and now you've got to learn three types of symmetry — but don't worry, I reckon their names pretty much give the game away.

There are THREE types of symmetry:	
1) LINE SYMMETRY	You can draw a mirror line across the object and both sides will fold together exactly.
2) PLANE SYMMETRY	This applies to 3-D solids. You can draw a plane mirror surface through the solid to make the shape exactly the same on both sides of the plane.
3) ROTATIONAL SYMMETRY	You can rotate the shape or drawing into different positions that all look exactly the same.

Q1 Draw all the lines of symmetry for each of the following shapes.
(Some shapes may have no lines of symmetry)

a)   b)   c)   d)   e)   f)

These questions are a piece of cake if you use tracing paper — and remember you can use it in the Exam, so take some with you or ask for it.

Q2 What is the order of rotational symmetry for each of the following shapes?

a)   b)   c)   d)

Q3 Mark in the lines of symmetry of the following letters. State the order of rotational symmetry for each one.

MHVBAKSZ

UNIT FOUR

Symmetry

 Watch out for those 3-D solids and planes of symmetry — they're pretty hard to draw, so make sure you do this page in pencil — and have a rubber ready...

Q4 Draw an example of each of the following shapes. Put in the <u>axes of symmetry</u> and state the <u>order</u> of rotational symmetry.

    a) An equilateral triangle.   **d)** An isosceles trapezium.
    b) An isosceles triangle.   **e)** A regular octagon.
    c) A rhombus.   **f)** A parallelogram.

Q5 On each cube draw in a different <u>plane of symmetry</u>.

Q6 Here is a cuboid: Is the plane a plane of symmetry?

Q7 How many planes of symmetry does this <u>triangular prism</u> have?

Q8 How many planes of symmetry does a <u>circular cone</u> have?

Q9 In the square based pyramid shown, is this a plane of symmetry?

Q10 Draw in another plane of symmetry, which is <u>perpendicular</u> to the one drawn in the diagram.

Unit Four

The Four Transformations

   Only 4 of these to learn... and good old TERRY's always around to help if you need him.

Q1 Copy the axes and mark on triangle A with corners (-1, 2), (0, 4) and (-2, 4).

Use a scale of 1 cm to 1 unit.

a) Reflect A in the line $y = -x$. Label this image B.
b) Reflect A in the line $x = 1$. Label the image C.
c) Reflect A in the line $y = -1$. Label the image D.
d) Translate triangle D with the vector $\begin{pmatrix} 4 \\ 2 \end{pmatrix}$. Label this image E.
e) Translate triangle C with the vector $\begin{pmatrix} 3 \\ -3 \end{pmatrix}$. Label this image F.
f) Describe fully the transformation that sends C to E.

It helps to label the corners of the triangle so you can see exactly what goes where when you do the transformations.

Transformations... just about the most fun you can have without crying.

Q2 Copy the axes using a scale of 1 cm to 1 unit. Mark on the axes a quadrilateral Q with corners (-2, 1), (-3, 1), (-3, 3) and (-2, 3).

a) Rotate Q clockwise through 90° about the point (-1, 2). Label the image R.
b) Rotate R clockwise through 90° about the point (0, 1). Label the image S.
c) Describe fully the rotation that maps Q to S.
d) Rotate Q through 180° about the point (-½, -1). Label the image T.
e) Rotate Q anticlockwise through 90° about the point (-1, -1). Label the image U.
f) Describe fully the rotation that sends U to T.

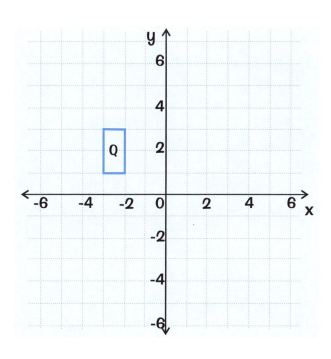

UNIT FOUR

The Four Transformations

Move each point separately — then check your shape hasn't done anything unexpected while you weren't looking.

Q3 Copy the axes below using a scale of 1 cm to 1 unit.

A parallelogram A has vertices at (6, 4), (10, 4), (8, 10) and (12, 10). Draw this parallelogram onto your axes. An enlargement scale factor ½ and centre (0,0) transforms parallelogram A onto its image B.

a) Draw this image B on your axes.

b) Translate B by the vector $\begin{pmatrix} -3 \\ -2 \end{pmatrix}$ and label this image C.

c) Calculate the ratio of the area of parallelogram C to the area of parallelogram A.

Q4 In the diagram, A is the point (4, 3), B is (4, 1) and C is (5, 1).

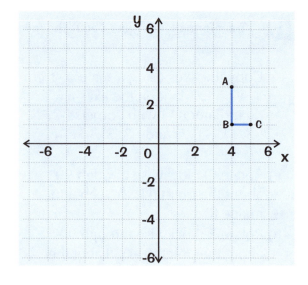

a) Using a scale of 1cm to 1 unit draw the diagram and mark on it the figure given by ABC.

b) Reflect ABC in the x-axis and label the image $A_1B_1C_1$.

c) Reflect $A_1B_1C_1$ in the y-axis and label the image $A_2B_2C_2$.

d) Describe fully the single transformation which would map ABC onto $A_2B_2C_2$.

Q5 Draw axes with x and y running from 0 to 12 with a scale of 1 cm to 1 unit.

O is the origin. $\vec{OP} = \begin{pmatrix} 4 \\ 2 \end{pmatrix}$, $\vec{PQ} = \begin{pmatrix} -1 \\ 2 \end{pmatrix}$, and $\vec{QR} = 2\vec{OP}$.

a) Mark P, Q and R on your axes.
b) Calculate the lengths of the vectors $\vec{OP}$ and $\vec{OQ}$.
c) Find the equation of the line joining P and Q.
d) Give R the translation $\vec{QO}$. Label the image T.
e) Verify that $\vec{PQ} + \vec{QR} + \vec{RT} + \vec{TP} = O$.

Urghh — vectors... Make sure you get the coordinates the right way round — top for x dir^n, bottom for y dir^n.

Pythagoras and Bearings

Don't try and do it all in your head — you've got to label the sides or you're bound to mess it up. Go on, get your pen out...

Q1 Find the unknown length in each of the following triangles.

It's easy to get lost if you don't follow the easy rules: always measure bearings from the <u>North Line</u> and always measure <u>Clockwise</u>.

Q2 Find the bearings required in these diagrams.

Q3 A walker travels 1200 m on a bearing of 165° and then another 1500 m on a bearing of 210°. By accurate measurement find how far she is now from her starting point. What bearing must she walk on to return to base?

Q4 A plane flies due east for 153 km then turns and flies due north for 116 km. How far is it now from where it started?

Q5 A coastguard spots a boat on a bearing of 040° and at a distance of 350 m. He can also see a tree due east of him. If the tree is due south of the boat, draw a diagram and measure accurately the distances of the:
  a) boat to the tree
  b) coastguard to the tree.
  c) Check by Pythagoras to see if your answers are reasonable.

Q6 a) Calculate the lengths WY and ZY.
  b) What is the total distance WXYZW?
  c) What is the area of quadrilateral WXYZ?

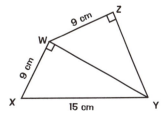

Unit Four

Pythagoras and Coordinates

Q1 Find the length of each of the lines on this graph.

Q2 The coordinates of four points are A(2,1), B(6,4), C(7,0) and D(3,–3). Calculate the distances:
a) AB   b) BC   c) CD   d) BD   e) AC
f) What shape is ABCD?

ahh... nice 'n' easy...

Q3 A square tablecloth has a diagonal measurement of 130 cm. What is the length of one side?

Q4 Find the length of line MN, where M and N have coordinates:
a) M(6,3) N(2,8)
b) M(1,5) N(8,12)
c) M(0,1) N(7,3)
d) M(9,5) N(4,8)
e) M(10,4) N(10,0)
f) M(12,6) N(13,0)

Q5 Find the length of line PQ, where P and Q have coordinates:
a) P(2,–3) Q(3,0)
b) P(1,–8) Q(4,3)
c) P(0,–1) Q(2,–3)
d) P(–6,–1) Q(7,–9)
e) P(12,–3) Q(–5,5)
f) P(–10,–2) Q(–2,–8)

OK, so there's a few negative numbers creeping in here, but just do them in the same way.

Q6 A flagpole 10 m high is supported by metal wires each 11 m long. How far from the foot of the pole must the wires be fastened to the ground if the other end is attached to the top of the pole?

UNIT FOUR

Trigonometry

Before you start a trigonometry question, write down the ratios, using SOH CAH TOA (Sockatoa!) — it'll help you pick your formula triangle.

Q1 Calculate the tan, sin and cos of each of these angles:
a) 17°   b) 83°   c) 5°   d) 28°   e) 45°.

Q2 Use the tangent ratio to find the unknowns:

Q3 Use the cosine ratio to find the unknowns:

Q4 Use the sine ratio to find the unknowns:

Q5 Find the unknowns using the appropriate ratios:

Q6 Calculate the height of the tree using the measurements in the diagram.

UNIT FOUR

Trigonometry

Q7 A boat travels 9 km due south and then 7 km due east. What bearing must it travel on to return to base?

Q8 This isosceles triangle has a base of 28 cm and a top angle of 54°. Calculate:

a) the length of sides AC and BC
b) the perpendicular height to C
c) the area of the triangle.

Make sure you've got the hang of the inverse SIN, COS and TAN functions on your calc... and check it's in DEG mode or you'll get nowhere fast.

Q9 An isosceles triangle has two equal sides of 7 cm and an angle between them of 65°. Calculate the area of the triangle.

Q10 In this parallelogram the diagonal CB is at right angles to AC. AB is 9.5 cm and ∠CAB is 60°. Calculate:

a) CB b) BD c) the area of the parallelogram.

Q11 This rhombus WXYZ has base 15 cm and diagonal WY of 28 cm. Calculate the:

a) length of diagonal XZ
b) area of the rhombus
c) angle WY makes with WX.

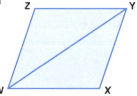

Q12 Two mountains are 1020 m and 1235 m high. Standing on the summit of the lower one I look up through an angle of elevation of 16° to see the summit of the higher one. Calculate the horizontal distance between the two mountains.

Q13 A girl is flying a kite. She holds the string, which is 45 m long, at a height of 1.3 m above the ground. The string of the kite makes an angle of 33° with the horizontal. What is the vertical height of the kite from the ground?

Q14 I am standing on top of an 80 m high tower. I look due north and see two cars with angles of depression of 38° and 49°. Calculate:

a) how far each car is from the base of the tower
b) how far apart the cars are.

Q15 A ship sails on a bearing of 300° for 100 km. The captain can then see a lighthouse due south of him that he knows is due west of his starting point. Calculate how far west the lighthouse is from the ship's starting point.

Unit Four

The Sine and Cosine Rules

Make sure you know the Sine Rule and <u>both forms</u> of the Cosine Rule. The one to use depends on which angles and sides you're given.

Q1 Calculate the lengths required to 3 s.f.

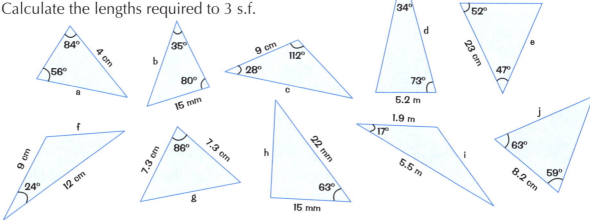

Q2 Calculate the angles required, to the nearest degree.

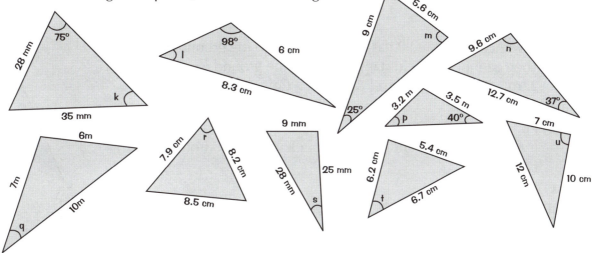

Q3 Calculate the lettered sides and angles.

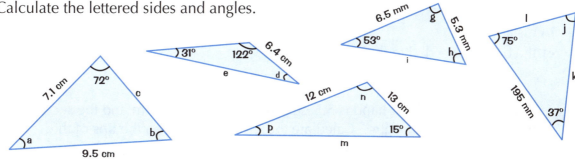

Q4 This field has measurements as shown. Calculate:
a) $\angle ZXY$
b) $\angle XYZ$
c) $\angle YZX$.

UNIT FOUR

The Sine and Cosine Rules

Q5 Peter is standing on a bridge over a river. He can see a tree on each bank, one 33 m and the other 35 m away from him. If he looks through an angle of 20° going from one tree to the other, how far apart are the two trees?

Q6 A coastguard sees a boat on a bearing of 038° from him and 25 km away. He also sees a ship 42 km away and on a bearing of 080°. Calculate:
  a) the distance of the boat from the ship
  b) the bearing of the boat from the ship.

Q7 An isosceles triangle has equal sides of length 7.5 cm and an angle of 56°. Sketch two possible triangles using this information and calculate the two possible lengths of the third side.

Q8 A parallelogram has sides of length 8 cm and 4.5 cm. One angle of the parallelogram is 124°. Calculate the lengths of the two diagonals.

Q9 A vertical flagpole FP has two stay wires to the ground at A and B. They cannot be equidistant from P, as the ground is uneven. AB is 22m, ∠PAB is 34° and ∠PBA is 50°. Calculate the distances:
  a) PA
  b) PB.
  If A is level with P and the angle of elevation of F from A is 49°, calculate:
  c) FA
  d) PF.

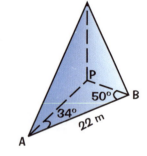

Q10 An aircraft leaves A and flies 257 km to B on a bearing of 257°. It then flies on to C, 215 km away on a bearing of 163° from B. Calculate:
  a) ∠ABC
  b) distance CA
  c) the bearing needed to fly from A direct to C.

Q11 On my clock the hour hand is 5.5 cm, the minute hand 8 cm and the second hand 7 cm, measured from the centre. Calculate the distance between the tips of the:
  a) hour and minute hands at 10 o'clock
  b) minute and second hands 15 seconds before 20 past the hour
  c) hour and minute hands at 1020.

So the minute hand is at 19.75 minutes past the hour.

Q12 Mary and Jane were standing one behind the other, 2.3 m apart, each holding one of the two strings of a kite flying directly in front of them. The angles of elevation of the kite from the girls were 65° and 48° respectively. Assuming the ends of both strings are held at the same height above the ground, calculate the length of each string.

UNIT FOUR

3D Pythagoras and Trigonometry

Q1
This rectangular box is 20 cm by 12 cm by 9 cm. Calculate:
a) angle ABE
b) length AF
c) length DF
d) angle EBH.

Q2 This pyramid is on a square base of side 56 cm. Its vertical height is 32 cm. Calculate the length of:
a) the line from E to the mid-point of BC
b) the sloping edge BE.

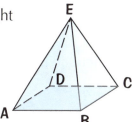

Q3 A rectangular box measures 20 cm by 30 cm by 8 cm. Calculate the lengths of:
a) the diagonal of each rectangular face
b) the diagonal through the centre of the box.

Q4 This glass has a radius of 2.8 cm. The straw in the glass makes an angle of 70° with the base and protrudes 4 cm above the rim.
a) How tall is the glass?
b) How long is the straw?

Q5 This cone has a perpendicular height of 9 cm. The centre of the base is O. The slant line from X makes an angle of 23° with the central axis. Calculate:
a) the radius of the base
b) the area of the base
c) the volume of the cone.

UNIT FOUR

Vectors

Q1 ABCDE is a pentagon.

$\vec{AB} = \begin{pmatrix} 3 \\ 3 \end{pmatrix}$ $\vec{AC} = \begin{pmatrix} 2 \\ 6 \end{pmatrix}$ $\vec{AD} = \begin{pmatrix} -2 \\ 6 \end{pmatrix}$ $\vec{AE} = \begin{pmatrix} -3 \\ 2 \end{pmatrix}$

a) Draw this pentagon accurately.

b) Write down the vectors:
  i) $\vec{DE}$ ii) $\vec{DC}$ iii) $\vec{EC}$

c) What sort of triangle is $\triangle$ ACD?

Q2 $p = \begin{pmatrix} 2 \\ 3 \end{pmatrix}$, $q = \begin{pmatrix} 0 \\ -2 \end{pmatrix}$, $r = \begin{pmatrix} 3 \\ -1 \end{pmatrix}$, $s = \begin{pmatrix} -1 \\ -2 \end{pmatrix}$

Calculate then draw:

a) $p + q$ c) $2r$ e) $2p - 2s$ g) $2r - q$ i) $p + 2s$
b) $p - q$ d) $s + p$ f) $3q + s$ h) $\frac{1}{2}q + 2r$ j) $q - 2r$

Q3

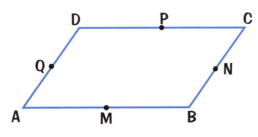

ABCD is a parallelogram. M, N, P and Q are the mid-points of the sides, as shown.
If $\vec{MQ} = x$ and $\vec{AM} = y$

Express in terms of x and y:

a) $\vec{AB}$ c) $\vec{NB}$ e) $\vec{AC}$
b) $\vec{AQ}$ d) $\vec{BC}$ f) $\vec{BD}$

Q4 In the diagram on the right, EB and AC are perpendicular. ABCE is a parallelogram. ∠EDC is a right angle.

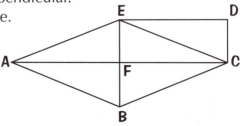

a) Name a vector equal to:
  i) $\vec{FC}$ iii) $\vec{BC}$ v) $2\vec{CD}$ vii) $\vec{EF} - \vec{CF}$
  ii) $\vec{FB}$ iv) $\vec{CE}$ vi) $\vec{AE} + \vec{EC}$ viii) $\vec{ED} + \vec{DC} + \vec{CB}$

b) If AC = 16 cm and EB = 6 cm:
  i) what is the area of ABCE?
  ii) what is the area of ABCDE?

Real-Life Vectors

Look at the pretty pictures... make sure you can see how this little lot fit with the questions.

Q1 In still water my motor boat can achieve 9 km/h. I aim the boat directly across the river which is running at 3 km/h. What is my resultant speed?

Q2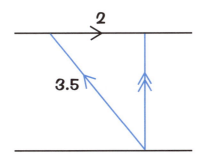

A girl wants to swim across a river running at 2 km/h. If she can swim at 3.5 km/h, calculate:

a) at what angle to the bank she should swim to go directly across
b) her resultant speed.

Q3 An aircraft is attempting to fly due north. It can achieve 600km/h but there is a wind from the west at 75 km/h, as shown. Calculate:

a) the actual bearing the aircraft is flying on
b) its resultant speed.

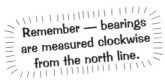
Remember — bearings are measured clockwise from the north line.

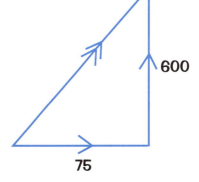

Q4 In the following diagrams, forces are acting on an object as shown.

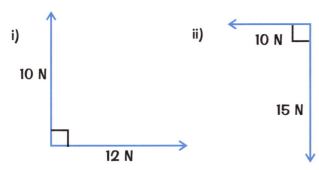

For each find:
a) the resultant force
b) its direction in relation to the larger force.

Put the vectors end to end and complete the triangle.

UNIT FOUR

y = mx + c

 Writing the equation of a line in the form y = mx + c gives you a nifty way of finding the gradient and y-intercept. Remember that — it'll save you loads of time. Anything for an easy life...

Q1 For each of the following lines, give the gradient and the coordinates of the point where the line cuts the y-axis.

I know these are a bit algebra-ish, but don't worry, they won't bite.

a) $y = 4x + 3$
b) $y = 3x - 2$
c) $y = 2x + 1$
d) $y = -3x + 3$
e) $y = 5x$
f) $y = -2x + 3$
g) $y = -6x - 4$
h) $y = x$
i) $y = -\frac{1}{2}x + 3$
j) $y = \frac{1}{4}x + 2$
k) $3y = 4x + 6$
l) $2y = -5x - 4$
m) $8y = 4x - 12$
n) $3y = 7x + 5$
o) $x + y = 0$
p) $x - y = 0$
q) $y - x = 3$
r) $x - 3 = y$
s) $y - 7 = 3x$
t) $y - 5x = 3$
u) $y + 2x + 3 = 0$
v) $y - 2x - 4 = 0$

Q2 What is the gradient of:

a) line A
b) line B
c) line C
d) line D
e) line E
f) line F
g) line G
h) line H
i) line I
j) line J
k) a line parallel to A
l) a line parallel to B
m) a line perpendicular to C?

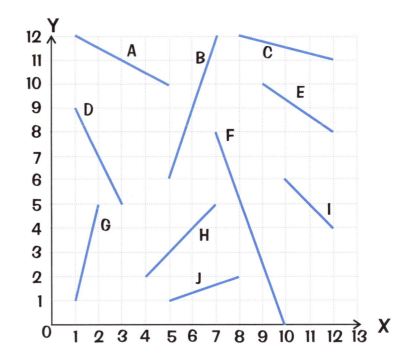

Uphill gradients are always positive, downhill always negative. Impressed? Hmmm....thought not. Can be a bit of an uphill battle, these.

Q3 What is the gradient of the lines joining the points:

a) (3, 5) and (5, 9)
b) (6, 3) and (10, 5)
c) (−6, 4) and (−3, 1)
d) (8, 2) and (4, 10)
e) (8, 5) and (6, 4)
f) (−3, −1) and (1, −4)?

UNIT FOUR

y = mx + c

Q4 Find the equation of the following lines:
a) A
b) B
c) C
d) D
e) E
f) F

Yeah, OK, this sounds a bit scary, but just work out the gradient (m) and look at the y-intercept (c) and pop them back into "y = mx + c"... easy lemons.

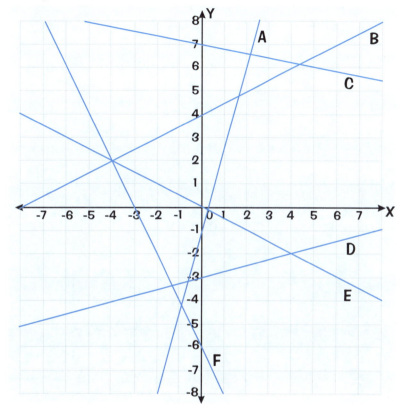

Q5 Find the equation of the straight line which passes through:
a) (3, 7) and has a gradient of 1
b) (2, 8) and has a gradient of 3
c) (−3, 3) and has a gradient of 2
d) (4, −4) and has a gradient of −1
e) (−1, 7) and has a gradient of −3
f) (4, −11) and has a gradient of −2.

Q6 Write down the equation of the line which passes through the points:
a) (2, 2) and (5, 5)
b) (1, 3) and (4, 12)
c) (−2, −3) and (5, 11)
d) (1, 0) and (5, −12)
e) (−5, 6) and (−1, −2)
f) (4, 23) and (−2, −7).

Here's a bit more practice with those gradients. Thought you'd like that.

Q7 What is the value of x or y if:
a) the point $(x, 13)$ is on the line $y = 3x + 1$
b) the point $(x, -2)$ is on the line $y = \frac{1}{2}x - 6$
c) the point $(4, y)$ is on the line $y = 2x - 1$
d) the point $(-3, y)$ is on the line $y = -3x$?

Q8 Which of the following points lie on the line $y = 3x - 1$?
(7, 20), (6, 15), (5, 14)

Unit Four

Graphs to Recognise

Q1 Here are some equations, and there are some curves below. Match the equations to the curves on this page and the following page.

a) $y = 3x + 1$

b) $y = 4x - 1$

c) $y = -2x - 1$

d) $y = -3x + 2$

e) $y = -2x$

f) $y = 3x$

g) $y = -x^2$

h) $y = x^2 + 2$

i) $y = x^2 - 3$

j) $y = -x^2 + 3$

k) $y = -x^2 - 3$

l) $y = x^2$

m) $y = x^3 + 3$

n) $y = 2x^3 - 3$

o) $y = -\frac{1}{2}x^3 + 2$

p) $y = -x^3 + 3$

q) $y = x^3$

r) $y = -\frac{3}{x}$

s) $y = \frac{2}{x}$

t) $y = \frac{1}{x^2}$

u) $y = -\frac{1}{x^2}$

i)

ii)

iii)

iv)

v)

vi)

vii)

viii)

ix)

 You'll need to be able to <u>sketch a graph</u> from <u>memory</u> — yeah, scary huh. Don't worry — they only expect you to remember the <u>4 main ones</u> (phew) — <u>straight</u> line (easy), <u>x²</u> (buckets), <u>x³</u> (wiggly) and <u>1/x</u> (2 bits and "x=0" missing).

UNIT FOUR

Graphs to Recognise

Solving Equations Using Graphs

Q1 Complete this table for $y = x^2 - 4$:

X	-4	-3	-2	-1	0	1	2	3	4
x^2									
-4									
y									

Draw the graph $y = x^2 - 4$
Use your graph to solve the following equations (to 1 d.p.):
a) $x^2 - 4 = 1$
b) $x^2 - 4 = 0$
c) $x^2 - 4 = x$

You're looking for the values of x which correspond to y = 1, 0 and x.

Q2 Use graphical methods to solve the following equations:
a) $x^2 + 3x = -2$ (use values $-4 \leqslant x \leqslant 2$)
b) $x^2 - 6 = x$ (use values $-4 \leqslant x \leqslant 4$)
c) $x^2 + 2 = x + 4$ (use values $-4 \leqslant x \leqslant 4$)
d) $x^2 + 7x = -12$ (use values $-5 \leqslant x \leqslant 0$)
e) $x^2 - 4 = -3x$ (use values $-5 \leqslant x \leqslant 2$)
f) $x^2 - 4x = -3$ (use values $0 \leqslant x \leqslant 5$)
g) $2x^2 + 5x = -2$ (use values $-3 \leqslant x \leqslant 0$)
h) $x^2 + 3x = x + 4$ (use values $-4 \leqslant x \leqslant 4$)

Q3 An object starts from a point O and moves in a straight line so that at time t seconds its displacement from O is d metres. The equation of its motion is given by $d = \frac{1}{2}t(5 - t)$.

a) Complete the following table:

t	0	1	2	2.5	3	4	5	6
½ t								
(5 - t)								
d = ½ t (5 – t)								

b) Draw a graph to show values for t from 0 to 6 on the horizontal scale using a scale of 2 cm to 1 second. Use a scale of 2 cm to 1 metre for values of d on the vertical scale.

c) Use your graph to answer the following questions:
   i) After how many seconds does the object return to O?
   ii) What was its greatest distance from O during the 6 seconds?
   iii) After how many seconds was the object at its greatest distance from O?
   iv) After how many seconds was the object 1 metre from O?
      (Give your answers to 1 d.p.)

UNIT FOUR

Simultaneous Equations and Graphs

Q1 Solve the following simultaneous equations by drawing graphs. Use values $0 \leq x \leq 6$.

a) $y = x$
   $y = 9 - 2x$

b) $y = 2x + 1$
   $2y = 8 + x$

c) $y = 4 - 2x$
   $x + y = 3$

d) $y = 3 - x$
   $3x + y = 5$

e) $2x + y = 6$
   $y = 3x + 1$

f) $y = 2x$
   $y = x + 1$

g) $x + y = 5$
   $2x - 1 = y$

h) $2y = 3x$
   $y = x + 1$

i) $y = x - 3$
   $y + x = 7$

j) $y = x + 1$
   $2x + y = 10$

Q2 The diagram shows the graphs:
$y = x^2 - x$
$y = x + 2$
$y = 8$
$y = -2x + 4$

Use the graphs to find the solutions to:

a) $x^2 - x = 0$
b) $x^2 - x = x + 2$
c) $x^2 - x = 8$
d) $x^2 - x = -2x + 4$
e) $-2x + 4 = x + 2$
f) $x^2 - x - 8 = 0$
g) $x^2 + x = 4$

 These equations look a bit nasty, but they're just made up of the equations you've got graphs for. And you know how to do the rest of it, don't you...

Q3 Complete this table for $y = -\frac{1}{2}x^2 + 5$:

X	-4	-3	-2	-1	0	1	2	3	4
$-\frac{1}{2}x^2$									
+5									
y									

Draw the graph $y = -\frac{1}{2}x^2 + 5$.
Use your graph to solve the following equations (to 1 d.p.):

a) $-\frac{1}{2}x^2 + 5 = 0$
b) $-\frac{1}{2}x^2 + 5 = -3$
c) $-\frac{1}{2}x^2 + 5 = x$

UNIT FOUR

The Graphs of Sin, Cos and Tan

 Remember — <u>Sin</u> and <u>Cos</u> only have values between <u>–1 and 1</u>.

Q1 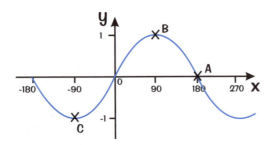 This is the graph of $y = \sin(x)$. Write down the coordinates of the points A, B and C.

Q2 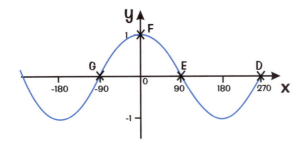 This is the graph of $y = \cos(x)$. Write down the coordinates of the points D, E, F and G.

Q3 This is the graph of $y = \tan(x)$. Write down the coordinates of the points H, I and J.

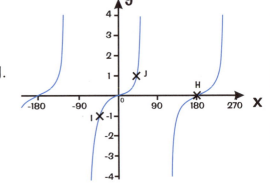

Don't forget — something strange happens with <u>tan</u> at 90°, 270°, 450° etc. — it shoots off to ± infinity... still, at least it comes back again (even if it is at <u>– infinity</u>.)

Q4 Which of the graphs $y = \sin(x)$, $y = \cos(x)$, $y = \tan(x)$ go through the points labelled A, B, C, ...J? (Sometimes it is more than one.)

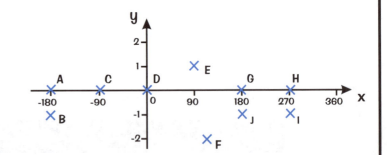

Q5 Plot the points given in this table.

x	0	90	180	270	360
y	2	1	0	1	2

Write down an equation for the curve you have plotted.

UNIT FOUR

The Graphs of Sin, Cos and Tan

Q6 For $0° \leqslant x \leqslant 360°$, draw the curves of:
  a) $y = \sin(2x)$
  b) $y = 2\sin(2x)$

Careful with these stretches — $\sin(kx)$ isn't the same as $k\sin(x)$.

Q7 Draw the curve of $y = 1 + \cos(x)$ for $-180° \leqslant x \leqslant 180°$.

Q8 Draw the curve of $y = -\sin(x)$ for $0° \leqslant x \leqslant 360°$.
What transformation is this of $y = \sin(x)$?

Q9 Draw accurately the graph of $y = 10\cos(x)$ for $-180° \leqslant x \leqslant 180°$.
On the same axes draw the graph of $10y = x + 20$.
Write down the coordinates of where the graphs cross. Show that this can be used to find a solution to the equation:
$$20 = 100\cos(x) - x.$$

Q10 Complete this table of values for $\sin(x)$ and $(\sin(x))^2$.

X	0	10	20	30	40	50	60	70	80	90
sin x		0.17		0.5						1
$(\sin x)^2$		0.03		0.25						1

Draw axes for the graph from $-180° \leqslant x \leqslant 180°$.
Plot the points for $(\sin(x))^2$.
From your knowledge of sin graphs, draw the rest of the graph for the limits given.

Q11 Draw accurately the graph of $y = \tan(x)$ for $0° \leqslant x \leqslant 360°$. Let the y-axis have values -12 to $+12$.
On the same axis, draw the graph of $10y - x = 25$.
Use your graphs to find an approximate solution to the equation $x = 10\tan(x) - 25$.

UNIT FOUR

Graphs: Shifts and Stretches

You've got to learn the rules for these shifts and stretches — there are only 4 types, so it won't take long. If you don't, either you'll have to spend ages working it out, or worse still you'll have to guess. Seems a bit of a waste of time and marks to me...

Q1 This is a graph of $y = f(x)$.

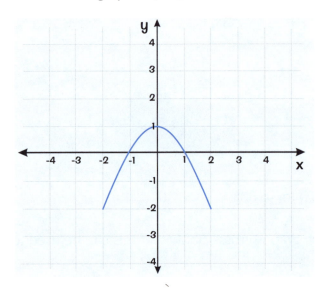

Use the graph of $y = f(x)$ to sketch:
a) $y = f(x) + 3$
b) $y = f(x) - 3$
c) $y = f(x + 3)$
d) $y = f(x - 3)$
e) $y = -f(x)$
f) $y = f(2x)$
g) $y = f(\frac{1}{2}x)$
h) $y = -f(2x)$

Q2 This is a graph of $y = f(x)$.

Use the graph of $y = f(x)$ to sketch:
a) $y = f(x) + 2$
b) $y = f(x) - 2$
c) $y = f(x + 2)$
d) $y = f(x - 2)$
e) $y = -f(x)$
f) $y = f(2x)$
g) $y = f(\frac{1}{2}x)$
h) $y = f(x + 3) - 1$
i) $y = f(x - 1) + 3$

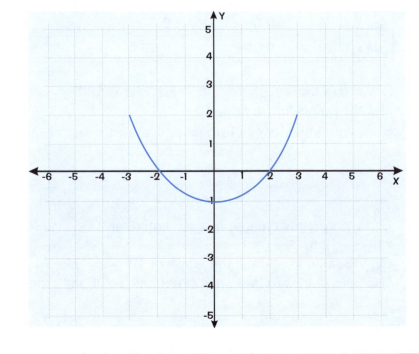

Graphs: Shifts and Stretches

Q3 This is the graph of $y = \sin(x)$:

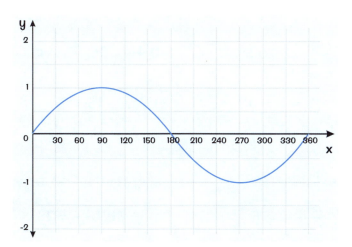

Draw the graphs of:
a) $y = 2\sin(x)$
b) $y = \sin(2x)$.

Q4 This is the graph of $y = \cos(x)$:

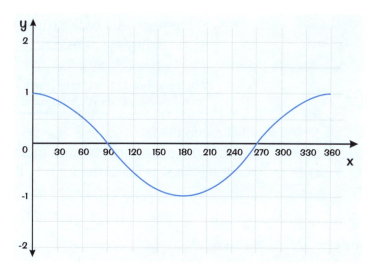

Draw the graphs of:
a) $y = 2\cos(x)$
b) $y = \cos(2x)$.

Q5 This is the graph of $y = f(x)$:
Sketch the graphs of:
a) $y = f(x) + 1$
b) $y = -f(x)$
c) $y = f(x + 1)$
d) $y = f(\tfrac{1}{2}x)$
e) $y = f(2x)$
f) $y = 2f(x)$
g) $y = f(x + 1) - 2$.

Phew — well, that's the lot on graphs... and what fun it was, too.

Unit Four

Solving Equations

Q1 When 1 is added to a number and the answer then trebled, it gives the same result as doubling the number and then adding 4. Find the number.

Q2 Solve the following:
a) $2x^2 = 18$
b) $2x^2 = 72$
c) $3x^2 = 27$
d) $4x^2 = 36$
e) $5x^2 = 5$

Q3 Solve the following:
a) $3x + 1 = 2x + 6$
b) $4x + 3 = 3x + 7$
c) $5x - 1 = 3x + 19$
d) $x + 2 = \frac{1}{2}x - 1$
e) $x + 15 = 4x$
f) $3x + 3 = 2x + 12$

Q4 Solve the following:
a) $3x - 8 = 7$
b) $2(x - 3) = -2$
c) $4(2x - 1) = 60$
d) $2x - 9 = 25$
e) $\frac{24}{x} + 2 = 6$
f) $5x - 2 = 6x - 7$
g) $30 - \frac{x^2}{2} = 28$

Q5 (x+1)cm

A square has sides of length $(x + 1)$ cm. Find the value of x if:
a) the perimeter of the square is 66 cm
b) the perimeter of the square is 152.8 cm.

With these wordy ones, you just have to write your own equation from the information you're given.

Q6 Mr Smith sent his car to the local garage. He spent £x on new parts, four times this amount on labour and finally £29 for an MOT test. If the total bill was for £106.50, find the value of x.

Q7 Solve:
a) $2(x - 3) - (x - 2) = 5$
b) $5(x + 2) - 3(x - 5) = 29$
c) $2(x + 2) + 3(x + 4) = 31$
d) $10(x + 3) - 4(x - 2) = 7(x + 5)$
e) $5(4x + 3) = 4(7x - 5) + 3(9 - 2x)$
f) $3(7 + 2x) + 2(1 - x) = 19$
g) $\frac{x}{3} + 7 = 12$
h) $\frac{x}{10} + 18 = 29$
i) $17 - \frac{x^2}{3} = 5$
j) $41 - \frac{x}{11} = 35$
k) $\frac{x}{100} - 3 = 4$
l) $\frac{120}{x} = 16$

Q8 Joan, Kate and Linda win £2,400 on the National Lottery between them. Joan gets a share of £x, whilst Kate gets twice as much as Joan. Linda's share is £232 less than Joan's amount.
a) Write down an expression for the amounts Joan, Kate and Linda win.
b) Write down an expression in terms of x, and solve it.
c) Write down the amounts Kate and Linda receive.

Q9 All the angles in the diagram are right angles.
a) Write down an expression for the perimeter of the shape.
b) Write down an expression for the area of the shape.
c) For what value of x will the perimeter and area be numerically equal?

Big blobs and broomsticks...

Solving Equations

Q10 Solve the following:

a) $5(x-1) + 3(x-4) = -11$

b) $3(x+2) + 2(x-4) = x - 3(x+3)$

c) $\dfrac{3x}{2} + 3 = x$

d) $3(4x+2) = 2(2x-1)$

e) $\dfrac{5x+7}{9} = 3$

f) $\dfrac{2x+7}{11} = 3$

It's easy — you just put the 2 bits together and there's your equation. Then all you've got to do is solve it...

Q11 For what value of x is the expression $14 - \dfrac{x}{2}$ equal to the value $\dfrac{3x-4}{2}$?

Q12 Two men are decorating a room. One has painted 20 m² and the other only 6 m². They continue painting and manage to paint another x m² each. If the first man has painted exactly three times the area painted by the second man, find the value of x.

Q13 Carol's father was 24 years old when Carol was born. Now he is four times as old as Carol. How old is Carol?

Q14 Mr Jones is 4 years older than his wife and 31 years older than his son. Their ages add up to 82 years. If Mr Jones is x years old, find the value of x and find the ages of his wife and son.

Q15 Solve the following:

a) $\dfrac{y}{2} + 2 = 13$

b) $\dfrac{3x}{4} - 2 = 4$

c) $\dfrac{2z}{5} - 3 = -5$

d) $\dfrac{1}{5}(x-4) = 3$

e) $\dfrac{2}{3}(x+1) = 16$

f) $\dfrac{3}{5}(4x-3) = 15$

g) $\dfrac{8}{x^2} = \dfrac{32}{36}$

h) $\dfrac{12}{5x^2} = \dfrac{3}{20}$

i) $\dfrac{14}{3x^2} = \dfrac{2}{21}$

Q16 A train travels at 70 mph for x hours and then at 80 mph for $3\tfrac{3}{4}$ hours. If the train covers 405 miles of track, find the value of x.

Q17 Solve the following: *Remember to do the same to the top and the bottom.*

a) $\dfrac{4x+3}{2} + x = \dfrac{5x+41}{4}$

b) $\dfrac{5}{7}(x-2) - \dfrac{3}{4}(x+3) = -4$

Q18 A triangle has lengths as shown below. Find the length of each side, if the length of AC exceeds that of AB by ½ cm.

Unit Four

Rearranging Formulas

Rearranging is getting the letter you want out of the formula and making it the subject. And it's exactly the same method as for solving equations, which can't be bad.

Q1 Rearrange the following formulas to make the letter in brackets the new subject.

a) $g = 10 - 4h$ (h)

b) $d = \frac{1}{2}(c + 4)$ (c)

c) $j = -2(3 - k)$ (k)

d) $a = \frac{2b}{3}$ (b)

e) $f = \frac{3g}{8}$ (g)

f) $y = \frac{x}{2} - 3$ (x)

g) $s = \frac{t}{6} + 10$ (t)

h) $p = 4q^2$ (q)

Q2 A car salesperson is paid £w for working m months and selling c cars, where
$$w = 500m + 50c$$
a) Rearrange the formula to make c the subject.
b) Find the number of cars the salesperson sells in 11 months if he earns £12,100 during that time.

Q3 The cost of hiring a car is £28 per day plus 25p per mile.
a) Find the cost of hiring the car for a day and travelling:
  i) 40 miles
  ii) 80 miles
b) Write down a formula to give the cost of hiring a car (£c) for one day, and travelling n miles.
c) Rearrange the formula to make n the subject.
d) How many miles can you travel, during one day, if you have a budget of:
  i) £34, ii) £50, iii) £56.50.

Q4 Rearrange the following formulas to make the letter in brackets the new subject.

a) $y = x^2 - 2$ (x)

b) $y = \sqrt{(x + 3)}$ (x)

c) $r = \left(\frac{s}{2}\right)^2$ (s)

d) $f = \frac{10 + g}{3}$ (g)

e) $w = \frac{5 - z}{2}$ (z)

f) $v = \frac{1}{3}x^2 h$ (x)

g) $v^2 = u^2 + 2as$ (a)

h) $v^2 = u^2 + 2as$ (u)

i) $t = 2\pi\sqrt{\frac{l}{g}}$ (g)

Q5 Mrs Smith buys x jumpers for £J each and sells them in her shop for a total price of £T.
a) Write down an expression for the amount of money she paid for all the jumpers.
b) Using your answer to **a)**, write down a formula for the profit £P Mrs Smith makes selling all the jumpers.
c) Rearrange the formula to make J the subject.
d) Given that Mrs Smith makes a profit of £156 by selling 13 jumpers for a total of £364 find the price she paid for each jumper originally.

UNIT FOUR

Rearranging Formulas

Q6 The cost of developing a film is 12p per print plus 60p postage.

    a) Find the cost of developing a film with:

        i) 12 prints.
        ii) 24 prints.

    b) Write down a formula for the cost C, in pence, of developing x prints.

    c) Rearrange the formula to make x the subject.

    d) Find the number of prints developed when a customer is charged:

        i) £4.92
        ii) £6.36
        iii) £12.12.

Q7 Rearrange the following formulas, by collecting terms in x and looking for common factors, to make x the new subject.

    a) $xy = z - 2x$
    b) $ax = 3x + b$
    c) $4x - y = xz$
    d) $xy = 3z - 5x + y$

    e) $xy = xz - 2$
    f) $2(x - y) = z(x + 3)$
    g) $xyz = x - y - wz$
    h) $3y(x + z) = y(2z - x)$

Q8 Rearrange the following to make the letter in brackets the new subject.

    a) $pq = 3p + 4r - 2q$ (p)

    b) $fg + 2e = 5 - 2g$ (g)

    c) $a(b - 2) = c(b + 3)$ (b)

    d) $pq^2 = rq^2 + 4$ (q)

    e) $4(a - b) + c(a - 2) = ad$ (a)

    f) $\dfrac{x^2}{3} - y = x^2$ (x)

    g) $\sqrt{hk^2 - 14} = k$ (k)

    h) $2\sqrt{x} + y = z\sqrt{x} + 4$ (x)

    i) $\dfrac{a}{b} = \dfrac{1}{3}(b - a)$ (a)

    j) $\dfrac{m + n}{m - n} = \dfrac{3}{4}$ (m)

    k) $\sqrt{\dfrac{(d - e)}{e}} = 7$ (e)

    l) $\dfrac{x - 2y}{xy} = 3$ (y)

These are getting quite tricky — you've got to collect like terms, before you can make anything else the subject.

Q9 Rearrange the following formulas to make y the new subject.

    a) $x(y - 1) = y$

    b) $x(y + 2) = y - 3$

    c) $x = \dfrac{y^2 + 1}{2y^2 - 1}$

    d) $x = \dfrac{2y^2 + 1}{3y^2 - 2}$

UNIT FOUR

Inequalities

Yet another one of those bits of Maths that looks worse than it is — these are just like equations, really, except for the symbols.

Q1 Write down the inequality represented by each diagram below.

Q2 By drawing an appropriate part of the number line for each question, represent each of the following inequalities.

a) $x > 5$
b) $x \leq 2$
c) $2 > x > -5$
d) $3 > x \geq -2$
e) $3 \geq x > -2$
f) $7 \geq x > 6$
g) $-3 \leq x \leq -2$
h) $0 \geq x > -3$

Q3 Draw and label a number line from –5 to 5 for each of the following questions. Represent the inequalities on your number lines.

a) $x^2 \leq 4$
b) $x^2 < 1$
c) $x^2 \leq 9$
d) $25 \geq x^2$
e) $16 \geq x^2$
f) $x^2 \leq 1$
g) $9 > x^2$
h) $x^2 \leq 0$

Q4 Solve the following:

a) $3x + 2 > 11$
b) $5x + 4 < 24$
c) $5x + 7 \leq 32$
d) $3x + 12 \leq 30$
e) $2x - 7 \geq 8$
f) $17 + 4x < 33$
g) $2(x + 3) < 20$
h) $2(5x - 4) < 32$
i) $5(x + 2) \geq 25$
j) $4(x - 1) > 40$
k) $10 - 2x > 4x - 8$
l) $7 - 2x \leq 4x + 10$
m) $8 - 3x \geq 14$
n) $16 - x < 11$
o) $16 - x > 1$
p) $12 - 3x \leq 18$

UNIT FOUR

Inequalities

Q5 Find the largest integer x, such that $2x + 5 \geq 5x - 2$.

Q6 When a number is subtracted from 11, and this new number is then divided by two, the result is always less than five. Write this information as an inequality and solve it to show the possible values of the number.

Q7 There are 1,130 pupils in a school. No class must have more than 32 pupils. How many classrooms should be used? Show this information as an inequality. *Call the number of classrooms x.*

Q8 A person is prepared to spend £300 taking friends out for a meal. If the restaurant charges £12 per head, how many guests could be invited? Show this information as an inequality.

Q9 The shaded region satisfies three inequalities. Write down these inequalities.

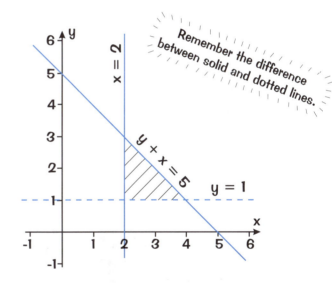

Remember the difference between solid and dotted lines.

Q10 Draw a set of axes with the x-axis from -2 to 6 and the y-axis from -1 to 7. Show on a graph the region enclosed by the following three inequalities.

$$y < 6 \quad , \quad x + y \geq 5 \quad \text{and} \quad x \leq 5$$

Q11 Draw a set of axes with the x-axis from 0 to 8 and the y-axis from 0 to 10. Show on a graph the region enclosed by the following three inequalities.

$$x > 1 \quad , \quad x + y \leq 7 \quad \text{and} \quad y \geq 2$$

Q12 Draw a set of axes with the x-axis from -4 to 5 and the y-axis from -3 to 6. Show on a graph the region enclosed by the following.

$$y \leq 2x + 4 \quad , \quad y < 5 - x \quad \text{and} \quad y \geq \frac{x}{3} - 1$$

UNIT FOUR

Factorising Quadratics

Q1 Factorise the quadratics first, and then solve the equations:
- **a)** $x^2 + 3x - 10 = 0$
- **b)** $x^2 - 5x + 6 = 0$
- **c)** $x^2 - 2x + 1 = 0$
- **d)** $x^2 - 4x + 3 = 0$
- **e)** $x^2 - x - 20 = 0$
- **f)** $x^2 - 4x - 5 = 0$
- **g)** $x^2 + 6x - 7 = 0$
- **h)** $x^2 + 14x + 49 = 0$
- **i)** $x^2 - 2x - 15 = 0$.

Q2 Rearrange into the form "$x^2 + bx + c = 0$", then solve by factorising:
- **a)** $x^2 + 6x = 16$
- **b)** $x^2 + 5x = 36$
- **c)** $x^2 + 4x = 45$
- **d)** $x^2 = 5x$
- **e)** $x^2 = 11x$
- **f)** $x^2 - 21 = 4x$
- **g)** $x^2 - 300 = 20x$
- **h)** $x^2 + 48 = 26x$
- **i)** $x^2 + 36 = 13x$
- **j)** $x + 5 - \dfrac{14}{x} = 0$
- **k)** $x + 4 - \dfrac{21}{x} = 0$
- **l)** $x(x - 3) = 10$
- **m)** $x^2 - 3(x + 6) = 0$
- **n)** $x - \dfrac{63}{x} = 2$
- **o)** $x + 1 = \dfrac{12}{x}$.

Q3 Solve $x^2 - \tfrac{1}{4} = 0$.

Q4 The area of a rectangular swimming pool is 28 m². The width is x m. The difference between the length and width is 3 m. Find the value of x.

Q5 A rug has length x m. The width is exactly 1 m less than the length.

- **a)** Write down an expression for the area of the rug.
- **b)** If the area of the rug is 6 m², find the value of x.

Q6 A triangle has height $(x + 1)$ cm and a base of $2x$ cm.
- **a)** Write down an expression for the area of the triangle and simplify it.
- **b)** If the area of the triangle is 12 cm², find the value of x.

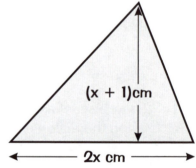

Q7 A square room has a floor of sides x metres. The height of the walls is 3 m. Write down an expression for:
- **a)** the floor area
- **b)** the area of all four walls.
- **c)** If the total area of the floor and the four walls is 64 m², form a quadratic equation and solve it to find x.

The Quadratic Formula

Q1 The following quadratics can be solved by factorisation, but practise using the formula to solve them.

a) $x^2 + 8x + 12 = 0$
b) $6x^2 - x - 2 = 0$
c) $x^2 - x - 6 = 0$
d) $x^2 - 3x + 2 = 0$
e) $4x^2 - 15x + 9 = 0$
f) $x^2 - 3x = 0$
g) $36x^2 - 48x + 16 = 0$
h) $3x^2 + 8x = 0$
i) $2x^2 - 7x - 4 = 0$

j) $x^2 + x - 20 = 0$
k) $4x^2 + 8x - 12 = 0$
l) $3x^2 - 11x - 20 = 0$
m) $x + 3 = 2x^2$
n) $5 - 3x - 2x^2 = 0$
o) $1 - 5x + 6x^2 = 0$
p) $3(x^2 + 2x) = 9$
q) $x^2 + 4(x - 3) = 0$
r) $x^2 = 2(4 - x)$

Step number 1... Write out the formula.

Step number 2... Write down values for a, b and c.

Step number 3... sub a, b and c into the formula. Be careful to divide the whole of the top line by 2a — not just ½ of it.

Q2 Rearrange the following in the form "$ax^2 + bx + c = 0$" and then solve by the quadratic formula. Give your answers to two decimal places.

a) $x^2 = 8 - 3x$
b) $(x + 2)^2 - 3 = 0$
c) $3x(x - 1) = 5$
d) $2x(x + 4) = 1$

e) $x^2 = 4(x + 1)$
f) $(2x - 1)^2 = 5$
g) $3x^2 + 2x = 6$
h) $(x + 2)(x + 3) = 5$

i) $(x - 2)(2x - 1) = 3$
j) $2x + \dfrac{4}{x} = 7$
k) $\left(x - \dfrac{1}{2}\right)^2 = \dfrac{1}{4}$
l) $4x(x - 2) = -3$

Pythagoras... remember him — you know, that bloke who didn't like angles.

Q3 The sides of a right-angled triangle are as shown. Use Pythagoras' theorem to form a quadratic equation in x and then solve it to find x.

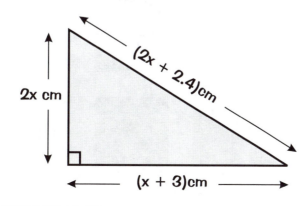

2x cm, (2x + 2.4) cm, (x + 3) cm

Completing the Square

All you're doing is writing it in the form "$(x + 4)^2 + 2$" instead of "$x^2 + 8x + 18$" — don't let the name put you off.

Q1 Complete the square for the following expressions:

a) $x^2 - 4x - 5$
b) $x^2 - 2x + 1$
c) $x^2 + x + 1$
d) $x^2 - 6x + 9$
e) $x^2 - 6x + 7$
f) $x^2 - 4x$

g) $x^2 + 3x - 4$
h) $x^2 - x - 3$
i) $x^2 - 10x + 25$
j) $x^2 - 10x$
k) $x^2 + 8x + 17$
l) $x^2 - 12x + 35$

First look at what you need to put in the bracket to get the x^2 and x terms. Then work the number part out at the end.

Q2 Solve the following quadratic equations by completing the square. Write down your answers to no more than 2 d.p.

a) $x^2 + 3x - 1 = 0$
b) $x^2 - x - 3 = 0$
c) $x^2 + 4x - 3 = 0$
d) $x^2 + x - 1 = 0$

e) $x^2 - 3x - 5 = 0$
f) $2x^2 - 6x + 1 = 0$
g) $3x^2 - 3x - 2 = 0$
h) $3x^2 - 6x - 1 = 0$

It's quite a cunning method, really... but I admit it takes a bit of getting used to — make sure you've learnt all the steps, then it's just practice, practice...

Algebra Crossword

ACROSS
1 Put brackets in (9)
5 You could do this to an equation (5)
6 There is a formula for this type of equation (9)
9 It goes with improvement (5)
10 Complete this shape (6)

DOWN
1 You should rearrange these (8)
2 $x \leq -6$ is an example of an _____ (10)
3 $2x + 4 = 6$ is one (8)
4 Some things grow, others _____ (5)
7 It's a type of proportion (7)
8 These are found a lot in algebra (and post boxes) (7)

UNIT FOUR

Trial and Improvement

Q1 The cubic equation $x^3 + x = 24$ has a solution between 2 and 3. Copy the table below and use it to find this solution to 1 d.p.

Guess(x)	Value of $x^3 + x$	Too large or Too small
2	$2^3 + 2 =$	
3	$3^3 + 3 =$	

Q2 The cubic equation $x^3 - x^2 + x = 7$ has a solution between 2 and 3. Copy the table below and use it to find this solution to 1 d.p.

Guess(x)	Value of $x^3 - x^2 + x$	Too large or Too small
2	$(2)^3 - (2)^2 + (2) =$	
3	$(3)^3 - (3)^2 + (3) =$	

Q3 The cubic equation $x^3 - x^2 = 0.7$ has a solution between 1 and 2. Copy the table on the right and use it to find this solution to 1 d.p.

Guess(x)	Value of $x^3 - x^2$	Too large or Too small
1	$(1)^3 - (1)^2 =$	
2	$(2)^3 - (2)^2 =$	

Q4 The cubic equation $x^3 + x^2 - 4x = 3$ has three solutions. The first solution lies between –3 and –2. The second lies between –1 and 0. The third solution lies between 1 and 2. Copy the table below and use it to find all three solutions to 1 d.p.

Guess(x)	Value of $x^3 + x^2 - 4x$	Too large or Too small
–3	$(-3)^3 + (-3)^2 - 4(-3) = -6$	
–2	$(-2)^3 + (-2)^2 - 4(-2) =$	
–1	$(-1)^3 + (-1)^2 - 4(-1) =$	
0	$(0)^3 + (0)^2 - 4(0) =$	
1	$(1)^3 + (1)^2 - 4(1) =$	
2	$(2)^3 + (2)^2 - 4(2) =$	

They don't always give you the starting numbers — so if they don't, make sure you pick two opposite cases (one too big, one too small), or you've blown it.

UNIT FOUR

Simultaneous Equations

To solve simultaneous equations from scratch, you've got to get rid of
either x or y first — to leave you with an equation with just one unknown in it.

Q1 Use the linear equation (the one with no x^2s in it) to find an expression for y. Then substitute it into the quadratic equation (the one with x^2s in it), to solve these equations:

a) $y = x^2 + 2$
$y = x + 14$

b) $y = x^2 - 8$
$y = 3x + 10$

c) $y = 2x^2$
$y = x + 3$

d) $x + 5y = 30$
$x^2 + \frac{4}{5}x = y$

e) $y = 1 - 13x$
$y = 4x^2 + 4$

f) $y = 3(x^2 + 3)$
$14x + y = 1$

Q2 Solve the following simultaneous equations:

a) $4x + 6y = 16$
$x + 2y = 5$

b) $3x + 8y = 24$
$x + y = 3$

c) $3y - 8x = 24$
$3y + 2x = 9$

d) $y = x^2 - 2$
$y = 3x + 8$

e) $y = 3x^2 - 10$
$13x - y = 14$

f) $y + 2 = 2x^2$
$y + 3x = 0$

g) $3y - 10x - 17 = 0$
$\frac{1}{3}y + 2x - 5 = 0$

h) $\frac{x}{2} - 2y = 5$
$12y + x - 2 = 0$

i) $x + y = \frac{1}{2}(y - x)$
$x + y = 2$

Careful with parts
d) to f) — some of
them are quadratics...

Q3 A farmer has a choice of buying 6 sheep and 5 pigs for £430 or 4 sheep and 10 pigs for £500 at auction.
a) If sheep cost £x and pigs cost £y, write down his two choices as a pair of simultaneous equations.
b) Solve for x and y.

Q4 Six apples and four oranges cost £1.90, whereas eight apples and two oranges cost £1.80. Find the cost of an apple and the cost of an orange.

Q5 Three pens and seven pencils cost £1.31 whereas eight pencils and six pens cost £1.96. Find the cost of each.

Q6 Find the value of x and y for each of the following rectangles, by first writing down a pair of simultaneous equations and then solving them.

Q7 Two customers enter a shop to buy milk and cornflakes. Mrs Smith buys 5 pints of milk and 2 boxes of cornflakes and spends £3.44. Mr Brown buys 4 pints of milk and 3 boxes of cornflakes and receives £6.03 change after paying with a £10 note. Write down a pair of simultaneous equations and solve them to find the price in pence of a pint of milk (m) and a box of cornflakes (c).

Q8 Solve $\frac{3(x - y)}{5} = x - 3y = x - 6$.

UNIT FOUR

Compound Growth and Decay

 Hey look — it's another of those "there is only one formula to learn and you use it for every question" topics.

So I reckon you'd better learn The Formula then...

Q1 Calculate the amount in each account if:
a) £200 is invested for 10 years at 9% compound interest per annum
b) £500 is invested for 3 years at 7% compound interest per annum
c) £750 is invested for 30 months at 8% compound interest per annum
d) £1000 is invested for 15 months at 6.5% compound interest per annum

Q2 A colony of bacteria grows at the compound rate of 12% per hour. Initially there are 200 bacteria.
a) How many will there be after 3 hours?
b) How many will there be after 1 day?
c) After how many whole hours will there be at least 4000 bacteria? (Solve this by trial and error.)

Just make sure you get the increase and decrease the right way round... basically, just check your answer sounds like you'd expect — and if it doesn't, do it again.

Q3 A radioactive element was observed every day and the mass remaining was measured. Initially there was 9 kg, but this decreased at the compound rate of 3% per day. How much radioactive element will be left after:
a) 3 days?
b) 6 days?
c) 1 week?
d) 4 weeks?
Give your answer to no more than 3 d.p.

Q4 Money is invested on the stock market. During a recession the value of the shares fall by 2% per week.
Find the value of the stock if:
a) £2000 was invested for a fortnight
b) £30,000 was invested for four weeks
c) £500 was invested for 7 weeks
d) £100,000 was invested for a year

Q5 Mrs Smith decides to invest £7000 in a savings account. She has the choice of putting all her money into an account paying 5% compound interest per annum or she can put half of her investment into an account paying 6% compound interest per annum and the remaining half into an account paying 4% per annum.
If she left the investment alone for 3 years, which is her best option and by how much?

 I'd put my money in Victorian rolling pins, myself...

UNIT FOUR

Compound Growth and Decay

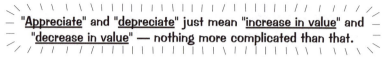

"Appreciate" and "depreciate" just mean "increase in value" and "decrease in value" — nothing more complicated than that.

Q6 An antique vase has increased in value since its owner bought it five years ago at £220. If its value has appreciated by 16% per year, how much is it worth today?

Q7 A company owns machinery which cost £3,500 four years ago. The depreciation has been 2½% per year. What is the machinery's second-hand value today?

Q8 The activity of a radio-isotope decreases at a compound rate of 9% every hour. If the initial activity is recorded at 1100 counts per minute, what will it be after:
a) 2 hours?
b) 4 hours?
c) 1 day?
d) The activity of the same radio-isotope is recorded at just 66 counts per minute. Using trial and error, estimate the length of time elapsed since the recording of 1100 counts per minute.

Q9 A car is estimated to depreciate in value by 14% each year. Find the estimated values of these used cars:
a) a Peugeot 206 which cost £8,495 six months ago
b) a BMW which cost £34,000 eighteen months ago
c) a Volvo S40 which cost £13,495 two years ago
d) a Vauxhall Vectra which cost £14,395 two years ago
e) a Ford Escort which cost £11,295 three years ago
f) a Daewoo Nexia which cost £6,795 twelve months ago

Q10 Property prices in one area have depreciated in value by 5% per year. Calculate the expected value today of these properties:
a) a house bought for £45,000, 3 years ago
b) a bungalow bought for £58,000, 4 years ago
c) a flat bought for £52,000, six months ago
d) a factory bought for £350,000, 7 years ago

Q11 A culture of bacteria increases in number at a compound rate of 0.4% per hour. If initially there was a culture of 50 cells, how many cells will there be after:
a) 3 hours?
b) 8 hours 30 minutes?
c) 135 mins?
d) 2 days?

Q12 The population of a country is 16 million, and the annual compound growth rate is estimated to be 1.3%. Predict the country's population in:
a) 4 years' time
b) 20 years' time

UNIT FOUR

Direct and Inverse Proportion

Q1 If 17 textbooks cost £150.45, how much will 28 cost?

Q2 If it takes 4 people 28 hours to complete a task, how long would it take just one person?

Q3 A person earns £6.20 an hour. How much do they earn for 15½ hours work?

Q4 On a map, 2 cm represents 3 km.
  a) If two towns are 14 km apart, what is the distance between them on the map?
  b) If two road junctions are 20.3 cm apart on the map, what is their real distance apart?

Q5 y is directly proportional to x. If $y = 5$ when x is 25, find y when x is 100.

Q6 y is directly proportional to x. If y is 1.2 when x is 2.5, find the value of y when $x = 3.75$.

Q7 If $y \propto x$ and $y = 132$ when $x = 10$, find the value of y when $x = 14$.

Q8 If $y \propto x$ and $y = 117$ when $x = 45$, find the value of x when $y = 195$.

Q9 Complete the following tables of values where y is always directly proportional to x.

  a)
x	2	4	6
y	5	10	

  b)
x	3	6	9
y		9	

  c)
x	27		
y	5	10	15

Q10 If $y = 3$ when $x = 8$ and y is inversely proportional to x, find the value of y when $x = 12$.

Q11 If $y \propto \dfrac{1}{x}$ and $x = 4$ when $y = 5$, find the value of x when $y = 10$.

Q12 If y and x vary inversely, and $y = 12$ when $x = 3$ find:
  a) the value of x when $y = 9$
  b) the value of y when $x = 6$

Q13 A man travels for 2 hours at 72 km per hour, completing a journey between two towns. Meanwhile another man completes the same journey at a speed of 80 km per hour. How long did it take him?

Q14 Given that $y \propto \dfrac{1}{x}$, complete this table of values.

x	1	2	3	4	5	6
y					9.6	

Put the numbers into the equation $y = k/x$ to find the value of k. Then you can find the rest of the ys.

Make sure you know the 4 main details about Direct and Inverse Proportion:
1) what happens when one quantity increases,
2) the graph,
3) the table of values, and
4) whether it's the ratio or the product that's the same for all values.

UNIT FOUR

Direct and Inverse Proportion

Q15 The area of a circle is proportional to the square of the radius. If the area is 113 cm² when the radius is 6 cm, find:
a) the area of a circle with radius 5 cm
b) the radius of a circle with area 29 cm²
(Give your answers to 1 d.p.)

Q16 If y is inversely proportional to the square of x, and $y = 4$ when $x = 6$. Find the value of:
a) y when $x = 3$
b) x when $y = 9$, given that x is negative

Q17 If $y \propto x^2$ and $y = 4$ when $x = 4$, find the value of y when $x = 12$.

Q18 $y = kx^3$ and $y = 200$ when $x = 5$.
a) Find the value of k.
b) Find the value of y when $x = 8$.
c) Find the value of x when $y = 2433.4$.

Q19 Given that y varies inversely as the square of x, complete the following table of values, given that x is always positive.

x	1	2	5
y		4	1

x	2		8
y	24	6	2⅔

Q20 Two cylindrical containers are filled to the same depth, d cm, with water. The mass of the water in each container is proportional to the square of the radius of each container. The first container has a radius of 16 cm and the water has a mass of 16 kg. If the second container has a radius of 8 cm, find the mass of the water inside it.

r = 16 cm

r = 8 cm

Q21 Given that r varies inversely as the square of s, and $r = 24$ when $s = 10$, find the values of:
a) r when $s = 5$
b) s when $r = 150$, given that s is positive
c) r when $s = 2$
d) s when $r = 37\frac{1}{2}$, given that s is negative

Don't forget about that little joker, the "inverse square" variation — they'll expect you to know that, too.

Q22 By considering the values in the table, decide whether $y \propto x$, $y \propto \frac{1}{x}$, $y \propto x^2$ or $y \propto \frac{1}{x^2}$.
a) Write down the equation which shows how y varies with x.
b) Find the value of y when $x = 6.4$.
c) Find the value of x when $y = 16$.

x	1.2	2.5	3.2	4.8
y	166⅔	80	62.5	41⅔

UNIT FOUR